KUSH
TO
MYSTERIOUS
BABYLON

The History of the Hindu Caste & White Privilege

2nd edition

By

Michael Ray Lemons

Library of Congress
Copyright Registration Number TX 9-503-356

Published by:
O'lemon & Underwood Publishing
379 North Oates Street
P. O. Box 95
Dothan, Alabama

Dedication

With deep love and eternal gratitude,

I dedicate this book to the memory of my mother, Mary Underwood Lemons.

Her stories of growing-up —woven with scripture, wisdom, and grace—inspired me to question tradition, seek truth, and explore history beyond what was taught in textbooks. Through our conversations, she planted in me a passion for American history, an appreciation for global cultures, and a reverence for the divine thread connecting them all.

Writing has never come easily for me. But some stories demand to be told.

And it was her voice—gentle, strong, faithful—that gave me the courage to tell them.

Thank you, Mom, for believing in me before I believed in myself.

This book is as much yours as it is mine.

Table of Contents

Acknowledgment

To the warriors of justice – known and unknown – who have stood against the tides of racism, oppression, and inequality: this book is your story too. As I wrote "Kush To Mysterious Babylon: The History of the Hindu Caste & White Privilege," I found myself walking in the footsteps of countless brave souls who came before me. Some of their names are lost to history, yet their impact echoes through time. These unnamed heroes who fought against bigotry and prejudice – your struggles light the way forward for all of us.

To everyone who shared their raw, honest stories with me: you breathed life into these pages. Your experiences, painful as they may have been to recount, paint a vivid picture of both our struggles and our resilience. Your truth-telling makes this work real, relevant, and vital.

I've been blessed with a family that understood the weight of this undertaking. During the long nights of research and writing, your patience never wavered. You gave me the strength to keep going when the subject matter grew heavy, and for that, I am forever grateful.

This book also stands on the shoulders of giants – the scholars, historians, educators, and activists who've dedicated their lives to understanding and exposing the complex web of racism, the birth of the Hindu caste system, and white privilege. Your research and insights have illuminated dark corners of human history, making our world a little more just with each revelation.

To the African Covenant People – humanity's first-born children, whose story runs deep through these pages: your journey, pain, and triumph are at the heart of this work. This book honors your endurance and celebrates your strength.

Finally, huge appreciation goes out to everyone, seen and unseen —who played a part in creating this book. We pay homage not only to our African Ancestors but also anyone of any race who works towards a more equal world.

From the depths of my heart, thank you all.

Michael Ray Lemons

Introduction

Why does skin color still define how we experience life—our politics, opportunities, and access to justice? To ignore the deep roots of racism is to ignore history itself. The global caste system, which ranks people by skin tone, origin, and status, continues to fuel inequality across continents. This hierarchy traces back to ancient settlers from the Balkans, whose ideas of racial superiority spread across India, Africa, the Aegean, and into the heart of the Western world.

These systems didn't just evolve—they were designed. Designed to control, divide, and dominate. From India's caste system to Europe's colonial regimes, the darker you were, the lower you stood. Those who held power uplifted themselves by dehumanizing those they labeled inferior.

This toxic mindset justifies cruelty against the poor, the colonized, the "other." It fuels conflict and division, and it's up to all of us to break it. We must challenge bigotry, dismantle institutionalized racism, and push for justice in every form.

One early example of racially motivated violence was the genocide committed by German forces in Namibia between 1904 and 1907. This atrocity marked the first state-sponsored genocide of the twentieth century. It contributed to the establishment of the term "genocide," derived from the Greek word "genos" (family, race) and the Latin "cide" (killing).

Over 60,000 Herero, San, and Nama people were slaughtered in what became the first state-sponsored genocide of the 20th century. This genocide set a precedent for future mass killings rooted in a racial hierarchy that dehumanized entire communities. The gruesome legacy included the transportation of skulls and human remains to Germany, where they were used to promote a false narrative of racial superiority, reflecting a chilling disregard for the humanity of the victims. Though Germany later acknowledged this atrocity, no meaningful reparations were made. This silence speaks volumes, reinforcing a pattern of historical denial and generational harm.

We've seen this pattern of colonial brutality before—with King Leopold II of Belgium, who's so-called "humanitarian mission" in the Congo led to the deaths of 10 to 15 million Africans. Under the lie of charity, Leopold built one of history's deadliest regimes—massacring villages, mutilating civilians, and destroying entire communities for rubber and profit.

Today, echoes of that cruelty are playing out in Gaza. Amid ongoing Israeli military assaults in Gaza and the West Bank, Israeli Defense Minister Yoav Gallant described Palestinians—

and Hamas fighters—as "human animals," while calling for the denial of basic necessities like food, water, electricity, and fuel to civilians. Human rights organizations across the globe have condemned these actions.

Since October 7, 2023—when Hamas launched a deadly attack—Israel's military response has killed thousands of Palestinian civilians, including many who were seeking humanitarian aid. According to UN reports, Israeli airstrikes have even targeted sites affiliated with the Gaza Humanitarian Foundation (GHF), an American-backed organization with close ties to Israel. But this violence is not new. It's part of a decades-long conflict rooted in the aftermath of World War II, when the state of Israel was established in 1948. Since then, Palestinians have faced forced displacement, military occupation, and ongoing disputes over land, borders, and basic human rights—all under the shadow of Israeli apartheid and settler-colonial expansion.

Even within Israel, scholars are speaking out. Omer Bartov, a leading Holocaust and genocide studies professor and former Israeli soldier, wrote in The New York Times that Israel's campaign against Gaza fits the definition of genocide. He joins a growing chorus of Jewish and Israeli voices condemning this long drawn-out war as a systematic campaign of mass violence.

This legacy of colonial violence doesn't end with the past. During both world wars, millions of Africans were conscripted to fight and die for European powers in wars they did not start. After the fighting ended, Africa was left behind—still colonized, still exploited. European empires, weakened but desperate to hold power, used divide-and-conquer tactics and brute force to control African nations.

But resistance grew. On March 6, 1957, Ghana became the first sub-Saharan African country to win independence. One by one, others followed. Yet even after political freedom, Western control remained—this time economic. Multinational corporations thrived on African instability, looting resources while ignoring infrastructure, healthcare, and education. In apartheid South Africa, racism was codified into law—another system where power was maintained by dehumanizing the oppressed.

Apartheid wasn't just a policy—it was a system built on the same caste principles that divided India and enslaved Africans in the Americas. Black South Africans were denied land, voting rights, jobs, and basic dignity. In Rwanda, Belgian colonizers deepened divisions between the Hutu and Tutsi communities based on false racial science, leading to one of the most horrific genocides of the 20th century.

When the world finally took notice in 1994, it was too late. Over a million people were dead. The United Nations failed to act. So did Belgium. So did the United States.

Africa's trauma is not just from colonization or slavery—it's from the constant erasure of its story, the stolen resources, and the lies told, about its people. From missionaries who came in peace but left behind soldiers, to slave ships that ripped generations from their homeland, the legacy of exploitation runs deep. But so does resistance.

Whether in the diaspora or on the continent, Black people have always resisted. In literature, in music, in movement. The fight for truth and justice is part of our DNA.

White supremacy was never just a belief—it was a strategy. It justified laws that banned education, ownership, and self-determination. It justified slavery, apartheid, Jim Crow, segregation, and colonialism. It built empires. It created economies. And it tried to erase every trace of African brilliance.

In Nazi Germany, these ideas reached genocidal extremes. Hitler's obsession with "racial purity" was partly rooted in the belief that Jews had African ancestry. Meanwhile, the United States and Western Europe built capitalist economies through more "refined" forms of the same racial caste system—slavery rebranded as mass incarceration; colonization rebranded as global trade.

The truth is this: Africa enriched the world. And the world robbed Africa.

Our story is one of brilliance, beauty, and betrayal. However, it's also one of survival, resilience, and hope. That is the purpose of this book. To challenge the lies. To connect the dots between the past and the present. And to call for a future built on justice, accountability, and liberation for all.

Africa Is Not Poor — It's Being Robbed

President Ibrahim Traoré of Burkina Faso made a powerful point: African students can recite scientific formulas, but they can't put them into practice—not because of a lack of intelligence, but because of a lack of infrastructure. That truth has sparked a new revolution. Small nations like Burkina Faso are leading the charge to reclaim sovereignty, nationalize their natural resources, break colonial chains, and forge new alliances with powers like Russia and China, while sidelining Western nations like the U.S., France, and the U.K.

Burkina Faso is not alone. Ghana, Niger, Mali, and other African nations are joining a growing movement to reject neocolonial control and reclaim their sovereignty. President Traoré has become a powerful symbol of this awakening—motivating Africans across the continent and throughout the diaspora to break the chains of oppression and pursue true self-empowerment.

Even European leaders are starting to speak the truth. In early 2024, Italian Prime Minister Giorgia Meloni shocked European elites by stating what many African nations have long known:

> "Africa is not poor. It is rich in resources and potential. What it needs is partnership, not charity."

Meloni called out the CFA franc—a colonial-era currency still used in parts of West and Central Africa—as a tool of French economic domination. In response, she launched the Mattei Plan, a €5.5 billion initiative aimed at supporting energy, education, healthcare, and infrastructure across the continent. Her stated goal: to empower African nations from within and reduce the root causes of forced migration.

But more striking was her public admission that many Africans no longer trust the West—and with good reason. She acknowledged that Europe has historically approached Africa with arrogance, exploitation, and self-interest, treating the continent as a supply zone, not a sovereign partner. Meloni admitted these policies have left behind a trail of broken promises and generational harm.

Her message was clear: if the West hopes to regain any moral or political credibility in Africa, it must abandon the colonial mindset and begin treating African nations as equals—not as charity cases or pawns in a geopolitical chess game.

While some African leaders cautiously welcomed the initiative, many warned Europe: We want real partnerships, not new colonial schemes.

Critics suspect Italy's plan may be more about securing energy deals and managing migration through authoritarian backroom deals, raising concerns about a new neocolonialism disguised as development aid.

But one thing is undeniable:

Africa is no longer begging. Africa is demanding respect.

Biblical Mark of the Beast (Revelation 13)

Definition:
A prophetic symbol in the Book of Revelation representing allegiance to the Beast—an imperial, anti-God system opposed to righteousness and divine justice.

Key Characteristics:

- Spiritual Allegiance: Those who accept the mark— side with a corrupt world order, rejecting divine law and justice (Rev. 13:16–17).
- Economic Control: Without the mark, people are barred from buying or selling—suggesting total economic exclusion.
- System of Idolatry: The Beast demands worship and loyalty, replacing God with state or imperial power (Rev. 13:8).
- Persecution of the Righteous: Those who resist the ideology of the Beast are hunted, silenced, or killed

(Rev. 13:15). In ancient Rome, crucifixion meant being nailed to a cross, a pole, or a stake. In the American South, public beatings and lynchings were tools of white supremacist terror. No one was safe—age, religion, and status offered no protection. Martyrs like Emmett Till, Dr. Martin Luther King Jr., Medgar Evers, Malcolm X, and Black Panther leader Fred Hampton—murdered in his sleep beside his pregnant fiancée, Deborah Johnson— were among many who were hunted like prey by an ideology rooted in fear and domination.

Symbolism:

- Forehead/Right Hand: Thought and action—total submission in mind and behavior.
- Number 666: Often interpreted as symbolic of human systems of domination (imperfection multiplied), especially oppressive empires like Rome. A new power— The United States of America emerged from Britain, inheriting the legacy of Rome and the British Empire. Like Rome, it became a symbol of military, political, and economic power. Its emblem—the eagle—echoes the imperial symbols of Babylon and Rome.

European Caste System (Post-Roman/ Colonial Era to Modern White Supremacy)

Definition:
A racial and social hierarchy developed through European imperialism, especially during colonization, slavery, and white Christian nationalism.

Key Characteristics:

- Racial Allegiance: Power and privilege reserved for whites; Black, Indigenous, and people of color are placed at the bottom of the hierarchy.
- Economic Control: Access to wealth, education, land, and citizenship is controlled through racialized laws and policies (e.g., Jim Crow, apartheid, Indo-European caste imitations).
- Cultural Supremacy: European languages, religions, features, and norms are made the global standard, while Indigenous and African ways are demonized.
- Persecution of the Other: Those who resist white supremacy face violence, economic retaliation, imprisonment, or death (e.g., colonized revolutionaries, civil rights activists, anti-caste rebels).

Symbolism:

- Colorism, Language, Lineage: Phenotypical markers become a social "brand" that defines one's place in the caste hierarchy.
- Citizenship and Belonging: Enforced by passports, bloodlines, ethnicity, skin tone, borders, and policing—marking who is "civilized" or "barbaric, or who is "worthy."

Prophetic Connection: Mark of the Beast vs. Euro Caste System

Both the mark of the beast and the Euro caste system are symbols of false loyalty and spiritual-economic domination. The mark is not merely a chip or tattoo—it is a system of allegiance to a global empire that exalts power, violence, and profit over justice, and mercy.

Likewise, the Eurocentric caste system exalts whiteness, colonization, and racial capitalism over the sacred dignity of human beings—especially those of African, Indigenous, and Semitic descent.

Theological Reflection and Resistance

Many Afrocentric and Indigenous theologians interpret the mark of the beast as symbolic of white supremacy, colonial Christianity, and capitalist empire—systems that crucify the poor, exploit the land, and erase the spiritual identity of oppressed peoples.

To reject the mark, then, is not only to refuse political allegiance to a government entity or empire but to stand with the God of liberation—to restore covenant communities rooted in justice, freedom, and dignity for all people — including the cast out.

Yeshua Ha'Mashiach—known in English as Jesus Christ— once said, "If anyone has ears to hear, let them hear." This wasn't just about listening with our ears, but opening our hearts and minds to deeper truths. Today, that message still calls out through the voices of freedom fighters like Dr. Martin Luther King Jr., Nelson Mandela, Medgar Evers, Harriet Tubman, John Lewis, and Frederick Douglass—all of whom warned the world about the dangers of caste systems and the idolatry of white supremacy.

These systems are not just political—they are spiritual. At their core lies a dangerous deception: the worship of whiteness as divine. This is what the Bible calls the Mark of the Beast—a false allegiance to power, control, and human domination in place of God.

We need more people, especially those within the white community, to reject this false worship, speak out, and help dismantle the myth of racial superiority. Whiteness is not divinity. The white race is not God. And until that truth is reckoned with, justice and peace will remain out of reach.

CHAPTER 1

The Legacy of an Ancient African Empire

Compared to the ancient names in Genesis' Table of Nations, the word Kush (also spelled Cush) refers not only to a person or ethnic group, but to a broader cultural and geographic identity. In the Hebrew Bible, Kush is identified as the son of Ham and the grandson of Noah. His descendants formed a powerful civilization known as the Kingdom of Kush.

Historically linked to present-day Ethiopia, the Kingdom of Kush extended far beyond modern borders, reaching into southern Egypt, Sudan, Eritrea, Somalia, and even parts of India. The Kushites were a dark-skinned people of advanced cultural, spiritual, and political development. They flourished along the Nile and across the Horn of Africa long before European colonization and the rewriting of African history.

The Book of Genesis offers one of the earliest references to the Kushitic people, identifying ancient Kush, often synonymous with ancient Ethiopia, as the first civilization mentioned in the Bible. Many scholars now recognize Kush as one of the oldest known civilizations on Earth, placing Africa firmly at the center of human history and development. Before centuries of erasure and Eurocentric distortion, Africa was understood to be what it truly is: the cradle of civilization and the birthplace of humanity.

In ancient times, many Kushitic peoples migrated to fertile regions around the Nile, the Sahara, and the Tigris-Euphrates River systems, becoming early hubs of trade, innovation, and cultural exchange. The Greeks referred to these African lands as Aethiopia, meaning "burned face"—a racialized term that reduced their dark skin to sun exposure rather than acknowledging it as natural and ancestral. This was one of the earliest examples of Eurocentric language used to distort African identity and diminish Black humanity.

According to Genesis, Kush was the firstborn of Ham. His lineage holds deep historical and theological significance. His son Nimrod journeyed eastward to build the first cities in the land of Shinar: Babel, Erech, Accad, Calneh, and Nineveh. These cities became early centers of empire and resistance against oppressive rule. While later Aryan religious interpretations portrayed Nimrod as a tyrant, the original texts—including the Epic of Gilgamesh, the Sennacherib Chronicle, and records from the Library of Ashurbanipal—depicted him as a strong leader and guardian of the Kushite region.

The Old Testament confirms the central importance of Kush by placing it near the legendary Garden of Eden. In the Genesis creation story, four rivers flow from Eden—Pishon, Gihon, Tigris (Hidekel), and the Euphrates. Notably, the Gihon River is said to encircle the whole land of Kush, reinforcing Africa's sacred place in the world's earliest cosmology. This stands in direct opposition to colonial narratives that have long painted Africa as primitive or irrelevant:

> *"Now a river went out of Eden to water the garden, and from there it parted and became four riverheads.*
>
> *The name of the second river is Gihon; it is the one which goes around the whole land of Kush."*
>
> (Genesis 2:10-14)

The Kushites share ancestral and cultural ties with modern-day Ethiopia and are regarded as one of the world's oldest and most influential African civilizations. Afrocentric scholars have emphasized the deep connections between ancient Kushitic peoples and today's East African cultures, especially in language, spiritual practices, and social structure. These ties center ancient Ethiopia not just geographically, but historically, as a foundational hub for global civilization.

The Birth of Civilization

Far from being on the margins, ancient Ethiopia was a beacon of architectural achievement, religious knowledge, and statecraft. Its influence continues to live on in the languages, traditions, and identities of East African nations, offering a direct challenge to the whitewashed histories produced through colonization and slavery.

A significant turning point came in 1974, with the discovery of Lucy—the oldest known human fossil—unearthed in Ethiopia's Awash Valley. Dated to over 3 million years ago, Lucy provided scientific proof that human life began in Africa, specifically in the broader Kushitic region. This discovery confirmed what many African historians and scholars had long asserted: Africa is not just the cradle of civilization but the birthplace of humanity itself.

Kush is one of the richest historical sites in Sub-Saharan Africa. It is home to thousands of pyramids built by the ancient Kingdom of Kush, more in number than those in Egypt. These monuments stand as a testament to a highly advanced society with deep spiritual and architectural knowledge.

Further north, the Great Pyramid of Giza remains one of the most iconic symbols of African ingenuity. Located on the Giza Plateau near modern-day Cairo, it is the largest of the three pyramids and the oldest of the Seven Wonders of the Ancient World—still remarkably intact. Built during the reign of Pharaoh Akhet Khufu (also known as Cheops), the pyramid was part of a massive funerary complex, including mortuary temples and tombs for royal family members.

Modern narratives often separate Egypt from its African context, but the pyramid-building tradition is deeply rooted in Nile Valley civilization. It spanned from the third to the sixth dynasties and was intertwined with the legacy of ancient Kush. These monuments in Nubia and Giza stand as enduring markers of a civilization whose contributions to science, architecture, spirituality, and governance helped shape the ancient world.

For centuries, the pyramids stood as the tallest artificial structures on Earth—monuments so mathematically precise and architecturally advanced that some have speculated they were built by extraterrestrial beings. However, such theories often reflect an unwillingness to acknowledge the brilliance of ancient African minds. The truth is, the Afrocentric civilizations of that era likely possessed a far more advanced understanding of science, engineering, and astronomy than many are prepared to admit today.

One of the most extraordinary figures of this golden age was Imhotep, whose name means "the one who comes in peace." Serving as vizier to Pharaoh Djoser during Egypt's Third Dynasty, Imhotep is widely credited with designing the Pyramid of Djoser—the world's first step pyramid—in Saqqara. He was more than just an architect: Imhotep was a polymath, revered as a physician, sculptor, scribe, priest, and astronomer. His influence was so profound that the Egyptians later deified and venerated him as a god of medicine and wisdom.

Together, King Djoser and Imhotep transformed Egypt's burial tradition. They began with the mastaba, a simple rectangular tomb made to protect the remains of nobles and royals. These structures were carved into bedrock, filled with masonry sand, and overlaid with large limestone blocks. The innovation came in stacking these mastabas vertically, layer upon layer, creating the world's first monumental pyramid.

Stones weighing tons were hauled into position by skilled laborers and workers, often wrongfully referred to only as slaves, using sleds, rollers, and advanced knowledge of weight distribution. Each block was precisely placed in horizontal alignment, revealing a masterful understanding of both physics and aesthetics.

More than just tombs, these pyramids were spiritual technologies, aligned with the stars and the sun's path. Like those that followed, the Pyramid of Djoser was deliberately constructed to capture the light of the sun's rays, symbolizing the soul's ascension into the afterlife. In this way, the pyramid became a tomb and a sacred ladder to the heavens.

The Pyramid of Djoser marked the dawn of monumental architecture in the ancient world, ushering in an age of innovation, spiritual expression, and statecraft through stone. Around its base, an intricate complex of artistry chapels, ceremonial courtyards, and funerary temples was constructed to honor the king and house the rites of passage into the afterlife. The structure began as a single-level mastaba, but layer upon layer was added—each smaller than the last—until the iconic step pyramid rose into the sky.

The outer surface was encased in smooth white limestone, gleaming in the desert sun. This design, resembling a staircase to the heavens, reflected the ancient African belief in the soul's ascent—a bridge between the earthly and divine. The Pyramid of Djoser was the first pyramid in history and a sacred symbol of spiritual and political power.

Inside, hieroglyphic inscriptions adorned the walls, telling vivid stories of royal life and national triumph. Scenes of military victories, wild animals, birds, lush vegetation, and everyday life—fishing, farming, hunting—were skillfully carved into stone. These engravings not only celebrated the king and his court but also captured the vibrant life and cosmology of the people.

Remarkably, many of these artistic masterpieces have endured nearly 5,000 years, maintaining their original form and aesthetic brilliance. The Kushite era, rooted in Nile Valley civilizations, produced more surviving monumental structures and artistic works than any other civilization on Earth. This enduring legacy is a testament to ancient African societies' genius, resilience, and cultural sophistication—a truth too often erased or diminished in the pages of mainstream history.

In Egypt, archaeologists have uncovered ancient documents written on papyrus, which are considered some of the oldest written records in the region. These papyri serve as a critical source of early Egyptian history, offering written accounts and hieroglyphic imagery that capture the worldview, spiritual beliefs, and daily experiences of those living along the Nile. They reveal insights into the construction of pyramids, agricultural cycles, religious rites, and the social order that defined Nile Valley life.

Among these records, the Kushites are prominently depicted in Egyptian hieroglyphs, recognizable by their dark skin, braided hair, and woolly textures, affirming their African identity. These visual and textual sources preserve the memory of Kushite presence and influence, which lies embedded in the earliest layers of Egyptian literature and culture. Before the rise of Eurocentrism, which later sought to disconnect Egypt from its African roots, ancient texts made no such division. The Nile Valley civilizations were part of a shared African legacy, stretching deep into Nubia and beyond.

The Nile, now celebrated as the lifeline of Egyptian civilization, was once uninhabitable until early African communities settled along its banks. These pioneers undertook the laborious work of clearing fertile land, constructing irrigation channels and dams, and developing agricultural systems that supported thriving cities. The Nile Delta, where the river empties into the Mediterranean Sea, became a hub of trade, culture, and communication, linking Africa to the broader ancient world.

As these civilizations rose, so did their intellectual, spiritual, and architectural achievements, laying the foundation for what the world would later call ancient Egypt. However, its roots are unmistakably African and deeply tied to the legacy of Kush.

No river on Earth has captivated the human imagination like the Nile. More than just a body of water, the Nile is a living artery of civilization, stretching across 11 African nations, from the highlands of Ethiopia to the vast Nile Delta where it empties into the Mediterranean Sea. Its two extraordinary tributaries—the Blue Nile, flowing from Ethiopia, and the White Nile, emerging from Uganda—converge to form a river system that winds through some of the continent's most diverse and fertile terrain.

From Lake Victoria's misty edges to Lake Albert's basin, the Nile carves its way through rugged mountainsides and swampy lowlands, navigating through a complex, interwoven network of streams, floodplains, and cataracts. As it passes through the deep slopes of the Rift Valley, the river becomes a source of life, sustaining herders, farmers, and wildlife. With each seasonal flood, the Nile deposits nutrient-rich silt back into the land, revitalizing the Nile Delta and fueling agricultural cycles that have sustained African civilizations for thousands of years.

The ancient city of Aswan, built on the banks of the Nile and facing south, served as a vital strategic and commercial gateway for southern Egypt. It connected trade routes from Nubia, Kush, and beyond, making it a cultural and economic crossroads. Further north, in Lower Egypt, the river's cataracts slowed just enough to irrigate the land, turning it into one of the most agriculturally productive regions in the ancient world.

The Nile has always been more than just a river. It's a symbol of renewal and resilience, shaping African history from Kush to Kemet, from ancient farmlands to the dreams of generations.

The ancient Kushites played a foundational role in the rise of Egyptian civilization. Far from being a peripheral culture, the Kushites were central to Egypt's political, spiritual, and intellectual development. In truth, Egypt owed much of its early advancement to Kushitic influence. The two civilizations shared a common ancestral lineage, which helped fuel the spread of Afro-Asiatic culture across the Nile Valley and throughout the Mediterranean.

Among Afrocentric traditions, Aswan—at the southern frontier of ancient Egypt—has long been viewed as a sacred site, perhaps the closest representation of paradise on Earth. Long before the Israelites reached the Promised Land of Canaan (Israel), they would have encountered the flourishing city-state of Aswan, a symbol of early civilization, divine order, and abundance. Its location along the Nile and its spiritual significance as a threshold between heaven and Earth contributed to its prosperity.

According to biblical texts, no human birth occurred in the Garden of Eden. Adam and Eve were exiled for eating from the Tree of Knowledge, and humanity's journey truly began outside that sacred space. In this context, the concept of the firstborn became central to the Covenant tradition. According to some interpretations, the earliest human birth is believed to have taken place in Aswan, connecting it to the idea of Pathros—Upper Egypt—as referenced in the Hebrew Bible. Pathros, which biblical scholars place in the region of modern-day northern Sudan (ancient Ethiopia), is thereby elevated as one of the most sacred geographies on Earth.

The Mitochondrial Eve and Our African Origins

Modern science confirms what many ancient traditions already understood: humanity began in Africa. The "Mitochondrial Eve" theory—based on mitochondrial DNA passed only from mother to child—shows that every living person on earth can trace their maternal ancestry back to a single African woman.

This discovery supports the Out of Africa theory, which holds that modern humans first emerged in Africa, most likely from the Pathros region (southern Egypt or ancient Nubia), before migrating across the globe.

Despite centuries of white supremacist ideology that has denied or distorted this truth, genetics proves that Africa is the birthplace of all humanity. And yet, the very continent that gave life to the world has been subject to colonization, exploitation, and racial dehumanization.

Understanding our shared African origin challenges today's global caste systems and racial hierarchies. It forces us to confront the injustice of white supremacy, colonial violence, and the systems built to deny the truth of our common humanity. The story of Mitochondrial Eve isn't just science—it's a call for accountability, historical truth, and spiritual reconciliation.

The Covenant made with the Israelites did not erase or replace the spiritual legacy of Pathros of upper Aswan—it extended it. While central to the Israelite narrative, Yahweh's blessings can be seen as a continuation of divine favor that had already manifested in the Nile Valley. Yet the Covenant came with a warning: it could be the greatest gift from God, or, if betrayed, it could unleash a series of devastating plagues and spiritual trials.

This layered legacy—linking Kush, Egypt, Aswan, and Israel—speaks to a much older and deeper origin story than often told, one rooted in Africa's sacred soil, and one that continues to shape spiritual consciousness across the globe.

Kushite-Israelite Ancestry and Division

The Kushitic people and the ancient Israelites shared a geographical proximity and a common ancestral lineage rooted in the sacred lands of Aswan, south of Egypt. For generations, Aswan was revered as the ancestral homeland of their forefathers—a source of deep spiritual pride for the broader Afro-Asiatic world. This sacred unity endured until new religious ideologies emerged from the Balkans, introducing polytheistic doctrines that fractured the spiritual and cultural ties between Kushites, Egyptians, and Israelites.

Historical memory among ancient Ethiopians and Jewish traditions reflects a shared reverence for Aswan and its role in the origin of the firstborn covenant. While the birth of Isaac introduced a new layer to the Abrahamic covenant, it could never replace the original Firstborn Covenant tied to the human family of ancient Aswan. The children of Jacob received an additional covenant, through Abraham, Isaac, and Jacob, that marked their inheritance of the Promised Land and identified them as a chosen people. Yet, this did not erase the foundational role of Aswan in the broader human and spiritual narrative.

The original inhabitants of Kush are widely believed to have spoken early Hebrew dialects, with Kushitic and Hebrew languages forming part of a broader linguistic and cultural family. Over time, many of these ancient tongues fell into extinction, along with much of the historical understanding that once bound these people together.

The eventual separation of the Kushites, Egyptians, and Israelites cannot be fully understood without addressing the stigma imposed by both foreign conquest and religious reinterpretation. These divisions were not organic—they were engineered, often rooted in colonial narratives, theological distortions, and racial hierarchies that served to disconnect Afro-Asiatic peoples from their shared origin and covenantal legacy.

Most Eurocentric writers have long distorted or outright erased the true identity of the ancient Hebrews, severing them from their Indigenous African roots. This deliberate misrepresentation has had a profound and lasting impact on how African peoples—and their central role in world history—are perceived. By removing the ancient Hebrews from the African narrative, these writers have obscured the deep spiritual, cultural, and genetic connections that tie the Afro-Asiatic peoples together.

In truth, humanity traces its origins to the Kush region of Africa. This sacred land, rich in history and spiritual resonance, is the cradle of civilization and the womb of holy memory. From the highlands of ancient Ethiopia to the banks of the Nile and beyond, humanity shares a common origin—a lineage that begins with the soil of Kush, long before the rise of empires or the drawing of borders.

Reclaiming this truth is not merely an act of historical correction—it is a spiritual restoration. It invites a return to the ancestral knowledge, sacred traditions, and divine order that once connected all people to the heart of Africa. The erasure of Africa from the biblical and historical narrative has done more than distort timelines—it has severed generations from their true inheritance.

But now, the memory of Kush rises again—a voice calling across millennia, reminding the world that the story of civilization does not begin in Europe or the Middle East, but in Africa, where the first humans walked, where the first kingdoms rose, and where the divine spark of humanity was first kindled.

I will bring back captives of Egypt and cause them to return to the land of Pathros (upper Aswan) to the land of their origin.

(Ezekiel 29:14)

Are you not like the people of Kushites to me, O children of Israel?

(Amos 9:7)

The Kushites established communities that evolved into thriving city-states, which became the backbone of an early governmental structure in Northeast Africa. Over time, these municipalities united, giving rise to one of the first great civilizations in world history. Long before the empires of Europe or Asia, the Kingdom of Kush stood as a beacon of cultural, political, and spiritual brilliance. Though its final decline came around 350 A.D., its legacy echoes across time.

Kush emerged as a vibrant hub for exchanging ideas among the ancient Ethiopian peoples. Here, advancements in agriculture, the science of iron metallurgy, art, religion, mining, and education flourished. The Kushites were among the first people to transition from stone to bronze tools, and they pioneered long-distance trade networks, reaching as far as India. They developed institutions of higher learning and created a system of governance and civil society that endured for over a millennium.

The kingdom had a succession of capitals in what is now northern Sudan, including the legendary city of Meroë—a center of iron production, architecture, and spiritual life. This cultural capital thrived until the fourth century A.D., when it was destroyed, prompting the Kushites to migrate northeast, eventually merging into the emerging Aksumite Empire in what is now Ethiopia and Eritrea.

No other ancient nation has matched the far-reaching influence of the Kushites in science, literature, religion, governance, and the arts. Their accomplishments were so profound that even the civilizations of Greece and Rome drew from their knowledge, artistic style, and spiritual systems. The

Kush's brilliance and ingenuity were not only miraculous but foundational, etched into the DNA of world civilization.

In the ancient world, Kush was a name known across continents. Its fame was widespread, and its people were revered. Even the Egyptians, in their earliest dynasties, were themselves descendants of Kush, long before waves of migration from the Balkans altered the demographic and spiritual composition of the Nile Valley.

The story of Kush is not a lost chapter—it is the opening line of humanity's epic. And now, it rises again.

The Kushites were among the world's earliest farmers, hunters, ironworkers, and master builders, laying the foundation for one of the most enduring civilizations in human history. The Kushitic Empire expanded its influence far beyond the Nile Valley, reaching into the Mediterranean and stretching across the Aegean Islands, leaving behind a legacy of ingenuity and abundance.

At the heart of Kushite society was a flourishing agricultural economy. They had total mastery over their environment, cultivating crops skillfully and precisely. Their fields produced wheat, barley, turnips, watermelon, cane, corn, lettuce, onions, garlic, and raw flax used to make fine linen. The fertile Nile Delta gave rise to some of the finest vineyards in the ancient world, yielding figs, blackberries, strawberries, mulberries, pomegranates, and grapes used to make wines for ceremonies, trade, and royal banquets.

The Kushites also excelled in hunting and fishing, living in harmony with their diverse environment. They hunted wild birds and large game—including lions, leopards, wildebeests, gazelles, oxen, warthogs, impala, sheep, and goats—while reaping the bounty of rivers, mountain streams, and ocean coastlines teeming with fish.

The climate of Kush provided ideal conditions for year-round food production and textile development. Within this thriving society, women held positions of high esteem. Female artisans played essential roles in the fabrication of garments, particularly for royalty and ceremonial life. Spinning, weaving, and clothing design were regarded as refined skills, and Kushite women were central to the empire's fashion, economy, and cultural expression.

With its influence spanning Africa, the Mediterranean, and parts of Asia, the Kushite Empire stood as a sophisticated and global power, far ahead of its time. Its achievements in agriculture, metallurgy, fashion, and international diplomacy formed the backbone of a civilization that empires like Greece and Rome would later emulate, but never truly equaled.

The Koran articulates the resentment between the human race and the chief fallen angel in the following passage:

We created man from dry clay, from black molded loam, and before him Satan from smokeless fire. Your Lord said to the angels, "I am creating man from dry clay, from black molded loam..." The angels, one and all, prostrated themselves, except Satan. He refused to prostrate himself with the others. He replied, "I will not bow to a mortal whom You created of dry clay of black moulded loam."

"Be gone," said God, "you are accursed, my curse shall be on you until the Day of Judgment!"

(Koran AL-Hijr 15:25-41)

"Lord," said Satan, "since You have seduced me, I will tempt mankind on earth; I will seduce them all, except those of them who are your faithful servants."

He replied, "This is My straight path, you shall have no power over My servants, only the sinners who follow you."

"I am nobler than he," he replied. "You created me from fire, but You created him from clay." He said: "Get down hence! This is no place for your contemptuous pride."

(Koran The Height 7:11)

Fallen Angels, Paganism, and Division

According to sacred tradition, in Satan's fall from grace, one-third of the angels were persuaded to join him in open rebellion against the divine order established by the Creator. These fallen angels were cast out from the heavenly realm and confined to operate within the unseen spiritual world. Yet their presence lingered, and over time, magic, sorcery, and idol worship emerged as human attempts to manipulate these immoral forces—forces that shared a singular goal: to disrupt divine harmony and inflict harm upon their enemies.

The fallen angels' strategy was subtle but effective: to lure humanity away from Yahweh by offering supernatural powers and mystical favors in exchange for devotion and ritual allegiance. Through idolatry, they forged spiritual contracts with humans who aligned themselves with their rebellion, promising access to hidden knowledge, strength, and influence in return for loyalty. Over generations, this dynamic between humanity and the spiritual realm evolved into elaborate mythologies—systems rooted in nature worship and cosmic dualism.

Pagan nations began crafting statues and images to represent their gods, building altars and sacred sites to honour these spiritual entities. The settlers from the Balkans, often identified with the early Aryan migrations, constructed grand temples for divination on the highest peaks and sacred grounds, establishing a visible hierarchy of worship centered on sky gods, fertility deities, and elemental spirits.

The melting of the vast ice glaciers that once covered the steppes of Europe reopened the pathways to the rest of the world. As these settlers moved southward and eastward, they carried their tradition and language, religious structures, and a sense of spiritual superiority. What followed was a long history of racial, ethnic, and religious divisions, often rooted in conquest, mythology, and the rejection of the original divine order known to the earliest African civilizations.

Satan, in his rebellion against the Creator, exploits human differences—racial, ethnic, and spiritual—as a means to implant his ideology and distribute power to those who align with his purposes. In scripture, he is portrayed as the great deceiver, attempting to redirect worship from Yahweh to himself, promising dominion in exchange for loyalty. This deception found fertile ground in many ancient traditions, including within the Hindu Vedas, where Aryan Gentiles are said to have accepted the invitation to serve the "gods"—interpreted here as cast-out angels—to establish a divinely sanctioned caste system.

This caste hierarchy was not just religious—it was racial. A Eurocentric value system emerged that weaponized spiritual superiority to devalue people with Afrocentric features, relegating them to second-class status. This structure was passed down through generations, embedded in strict Pagan protocols that mirrored the rebellion against God, systems designed to uphold racial stratification and spiritual deception.

In the Nile Delta, waves of Sea Peoples from the Balkans—identified biblically as the Philistines—invaded the land, displacing the covenant people and plunging their communities into chaos, symbolized as being "cast into a sea of fire." What followed was a spiritual wildfire: Paganism spread rapidly across Israelite and Kushite lands, burning through sacred traditions like flames sweeping in all directions, consuming altars, languages, and cultural memory.

For centuries, the Aryans were confined to the Balkan Mountain plateau during what could be considered their Stone Age, surviving with tools fashioned from bone and stone. In contrast, the civilizations of the Nile, Euphrates, and Tigris valleys had long since mastered metalworking, agriculture, and animal husbandry, establishing flourishing societies rooted in divine order and cultural sophistication.

When climatic shifts melted the glacial walls that once isolated the Aryans, they descended into lands already rich in knowledge and splendor. There, they encountered advanced African civilizations—people eating with utensils made of silver and gold, constructing monumental architecture, and adorning their homes with artistic and symbolic imagery carved into stone. The contrast was stark: where the South reflected divine creativity and spiritual alignment, the newcomers brought conquest, idol worship, and a racial ideology that sought to overwrite sacred truth with mythic supremacy.

In ancient times, the Nile River was the lifeblood of civilization, flooding the surrounding valleys each year between June and September due to the monsoon rains in the Ethiopian Highlands. These annual floods were not merely natural events—they were sacred rhythms that shaped the spiritual and agricultural life of the Nile Valley peoples. The Egyptians referred to the fertile region nourished by the floodwaters as the Black Land (Kemet), named for the rich, dark soil deposits left behind. In contrast, the arid surrounding desert was called the Red Land (Deshret), symbolic of chaos, barrenness, and danger.

The Nile could be both a blessing and a force of destruction. If its waters rose too high, the strong currents would sweep away fields, homes, and harvests, reminding the people of its divine power and the delicate balance between abundance and judgment. Yet for most of its course, the Nile remained a gently flowing river, stretching from the heart of Africa through the length of Egypt and anchoring one of the most enduring civilizations the world has ever known.

For the Kushite dominion, the Nile was far more than a river—it was a spiritual axis, a provider of life, and a corridor of culture and commerce. It was the backbone of their empire, linking the sacred lands of Nubia to the ancient cities of Kemet, and carrying with it the stories, songs, and sustenance of a people chosen to live in harmony with the earth and the divine.

The Nile River, the longest river on Earth, flows from the mountains of East Africa, carving its path through the continent with divine precision. Each year, it overflows its banks, replenishing the surrounding land before continuing its northward journey through the Sahara Desert and finally emptying into the Mediterranean Sea. Kushite civilization took root along its sacred banks, thriving in harmony with the river's life-giving rhythms.

Geological and archaeological evidence confirms that the Kushites established a habitable and prosperous civilization deeply intertwined with these flowing waters. The region's favorable climate supported agriculture, grazing, mining, and trade. The fertile plains, enriched by nutrient-rich silt from the Ethiopian Highlands, became some of the ancient world's earliest and most productive farmland. This land yielded precious stones, ivory, gold, and a bounty of crops that sustained powerful city-states and kingdoms.

The Kushites were not only resourceful but also artistic and inventive. They produced elegant clothing and pottery, and constructed lavish buildings using methods that reflected both spiritual purpose and architectural brilliance. The people of Kush mastered skills such as carpentry, masonry, weaving, and metallurgy, setting a cultural standard that would influence later civilizations.

Even Lower Egypt—often celebrated for its grandeur—was formed out of the black soil carried down by the Nile from ancient Ethiopia, a divine offering that brought life to a desert land. The Egyptians learned to build earthen dams and irrigation systems. Still, they owed their continued existence to the miraculous convergence of water and soil from the southern highlands—a gift of nature made sacred by the Creator.

As African settlers migrated along the Nile, they founded villages, which evolved into city-states, fortified with protective walls and sustained by advanced agricultural and engineering practices. Through their innovation, they achieved self-sufficiency and cultivated a civilization capable of supporting large, urban populations.

The Nile Valley was more than a source of survival—it was a cradle of civilization, a divine corridor that bore witness to the rise of African greatness. And at its heart stood the Kushites, a people whose harmony with the land, the elements, and the spirit marked them as pioneers of human progress.

In ancient times, the Sahara was not the vast, arid expanse we know today. It was once a watery and fertile region, filled with lakes, streams, grasslands, forests, and wetlands that supported abundant life. Stretching across a landmass nearly the size of the United States, this region served as a rich cradle of early African civilization.

Many Kushites settled along this lush Sahara and into the Mediterranean basin, bringing with them their extensive cultural knowledge, agricultural innovations, and systems of domestication. These early African peoples mastered the cultivation of rice, yams, wheat, barley, and other grains, long before large-scale migration began. They developed early animal husbandry, agricultural practices, and community planning skills that would later spread throughout the Afro-Asiatic world.

The ancient Sahara was a thriving ecological zone, a hub of cultural exchange and spiritual life. But over centuries, as the climate gradually shifted and the rains became scarce, the once-green Sahara began to dry. As grasslands gave way to dunes, many Kushitic and other indigenous groups migrated southward, toward the Red Sea, the Nile Valley, and deeper into the African interior.

This great migration helped disperse Kushite knowledge and customs across the continent, influencing civilizations far beyond their original homeland. Even in the face of environmental change, the legacy of these early African pioneers endured, etched into the land and preserved in oral tradition. It echoed in the cultural patterns of the regions they touched.

CHAPTER 2

The Kingdom of Sheba: Land and Legacy

The land of the Sabeans—known as the Kingdom of Sheba—was a mountainous and fertile region in southwestern Arabia, situated along the eastern shore of the Red Sea. This ancient civilization was ruled by the renowned Queen of Sheba, also known in Ethiopian tradition as Queen Makeda. According to biblical genealogy, Saba was the eldest son of Kush and the grandson of Ham, listed among the descendants of Noah in the Table of Nations in the Book of Genesis.

The capital city of Sheba, sharing the name Saba, was a thriving commercial and agricultural hub. It was located near waterways that nourished the land and allowed for abundant crop cultivation. These agricultural goods were not only consumed locally but also distributed throughout the greater Kingdom of Ethiopia, reinforcing the deep spiritual and economic ties between the Kushitic and Sabean worlds.

The name Sheba carries powerful spiritual resonance across both the Old and New Testaments. In the Gospels, the Queen of the South—identified with Sheba—is prophesied to rise in the latter days, and "will quickly stretch out her hand to God." Her legacy is one of wisdom, power, and spiritual discernment, revered for her journey to test King Solomon with hard questions, and her acknowledgment of the God of Israel.

In the New Testament, the Apostle Paul, after his miraculous encounter with Yeshua Ha'Mashiach (Jesus Christ), records in Galatians that Arabia, or Sabean territory, was the first place he journeyed to after his conversion. This underscores the spiritual and geographical importance of the Sabean region as a land rich in tradition, divine encounter, and sacred heritage.

Like other Kushite domains, Sabea was blessed with extraordinary natural resources and was a key player in the ancient world's trade networks. Its mountain slopes and coastal plains were home to trees that produced frankincense and myrrh—two of the most prized aromatic resins of the ancient world, used in religious rituals, medicine, and royal ceremonies. The Great Dam of Marib, which harnessed the waters of the Wadi Dhana, provided a sophisticated irrigation system, turning the arid land into a fertile and flourishing kingdom.

The legacy of Sheba is not just that of a wealthy kingdom, but of a people deeply rooted in the Kushite lineage, spiritually attuned to divine truth, and destined, according to prophecy, to rise again with outstretched hands toward the Creator.

The Great Dam of Marib was one of the most advanced feats of engineering in the ancient world. The Sabeans designed it as a complex irrigation system built with precision and vision. Composed of massive stones, earthen levees, and a series of canals, storage tanks, tunnels, and sluices, the dam efficiently captured and redirected rainwater and seasonal floodwaters for agricultural use. It transformed the arid landscape into fertile farmland, sustaining communities and cities for centuries.

The dam was more than a utility—it symbolized Sabean ingenuity, providing water for homes, public spaces, and even botanical gardens in the surrounding mountains. Aqueducts carried fresh water to support city life and agriculture through carefully designed networks that showed aesthetic beauty and scientific mastery. This innovation allowed the Sabeans to flourish in a harsh environment, and their cities became known for their prosperity, order, and luxury.

The monsoon rains from June to November were essential to this system. The Sabeans not only managed the floods but also harnessed the power of monsoon winds as navigational aids. These winds blew eastward toward India and the Far East and then reversed course, making them ideal for maritime trade. The Sabeans became master sailors, using the seasonal winds to establish trade routes that connected the Arabian Peninsula with India, East Africa, and beyond.

Their trade empire was vast and diverse. Sabean merchants exported cultivated grains, fruit, ivory, gold, silver, and rare spices. They were renowned for their production and trade of ginger, myrrh, frankincense, copper, glassware, dyes, silk garments, and ornaments adorned with exquisite stones. These goods were transported via camel caravans across the African continent and by sea vessels that travelled the Indian Ocean, making the Sabeans one of the most influential and wealthy civilizations in the ancient world.

Queen Makeda and the Divine Covenant

The Sabeans and their allies monopolized the flow of goods, ideas, and culture across the region by controlling key trade routes. Their wealth and success were not merely the result of location, but of their deep knowledge of nature, architecture, agriculture, and navigation, passed down through their Kushite heritage. Their civilization is a testament to what Afro-Asiatic societies accomplished long before the rise of Europe. It serves as a powerful reminder of the genius embedded in ancient African wisdom.

Geography was Kush's greatest defender. Nestled behind mountains, protected by massive dams, and guarded by the Nile's fierce rapids, the kingdom proved a nightmare for would-be invaders. The Sabeans learned this lesson firsthand during Augustus Caesar's reign when they raided Roman forces near Syene. What started as a Roman offensive ended in disaster—their troops, unfamiliar with the harsh terrain, were forced into the desert. There, the unforgiving landscape did what no army could, claiming the lives of countless Roman soldiers who died of thirst.

The Sabeans, an ancient people connected to the Kushites of Ethiopia, once returned victorious from battle, carrying a bronze statue head of Emperor Augustus Caesar—a symbol of imperial power.

According to both the Bible and the Quran, the prophets warned the Sabeans not to worship pagan gods. Disobedience, they said, would not only separate them from God spiritually but also expose them to insecurity, instability, and the loss of divine protection.

The covenant with God wasn't limited to Israel. It also extended to the Sabeans—descendants of the Kushites—who once lived across parts of Ethiopia and Arabia. These people were part of the Firstborn Covenant, a spiritual agreement requiring complete faithfulness to the Creator.

Like the Israelites, the ancient Ethiopians were expected to remain loyal to this divine pact. Falling away from it would bring judgment. They were promised protection and prosperity only if they honored the all-powerful Yahweh, who demanded justice, humility, and obedience.

This historical relationship mirrors today's struggles for justice and accountability. Systems built on privilege, colonization, and white supremacy often ignore the spiritual and historical roles of non-European peoples. But the covenant reminds us that consequences follow when power is misused or sacred responsibilities are abandoned. Rain is withheld. Plagues arrive. And former allies become enemies.

The story of the Kushites and Israelites isn't just ancient history—it's a call to remember the cost of disobedience and the need to dismantle unjust systems that betray divine truth.:

For the natives of Sheba, there was a sign in their dwelling: a garden on their right and a garden on their left. We said to them, "Eat of what your lord has given you and render thanks to Him. Pleasant is your land, and forgiving is your Lord."

But they gave no heed. So, we let loose upon them the dam's waters and replaced their gardens with two others bearing bitter fruits, tamarisks and a few nettle shrubs. Thus, did we punish them for their ingratitude? (Koran Sheba 24:15)

The waters will fail from the sea, and the river will be wasted and dried up. The river will turn foil...On the land of my people will come thorns and briers. (Isaiah 19:5)

Queen Makeda, better known as the Queen of Sheba, was undeniably from the Sabean region—an area deeply connected to the ancient Kingdom of Kush. While historical records don't clearly state whether she ruled the entire Kushite empire or just a portion, her legacy is linked to a time of both power and transition.

Before her reign, the Kushite kingdom had already suffered territorial losses along the Nile, including Egypt, which had fallen into the hands of invading Aryan forces. These Aryans destroyed key Kushite fortresses, forcing the empire to retreat further south.

Many historians believe Queen Makeda ruled from a palace in Meroe, the capital of Kush. According to the ancient Jewish historian Josephus, Sheba was not just a regional queen but the ruler of a unified Kushite empire. He described the prehistoric island of Meroe as a powerful city, encircled by the mighty Nile and flanked by two tributary rivers—the Astapus and the Astabaras—giving it natural protection and symbolic strength.

This historical account challenges Eurocentric narratives that downplay African civilization and leadership. The Queen of Sheba stands as a symbol of Black sovereignty, intelligence, and global influence, long before colonization or white supremacy sought to erase her legacy. Her story reminds us of the power once held by African women and the enduring significance of Kush in the broader history of human civilization.

In the Quran, the Queen of Sheba—often identified as Queen Makeda—approached King Solomon not for conquest, but to test his legendary wisdom. Her visit followed a divine report delivered by an unlikely messenger: the hoopoe bird, who informed Solomon about a powerful kingdom led by a queen who worshipped celestial deities.

The Sabeans had built a grand temple devoted to Ilumquh (also known as Sin), the god associated with the moon, Venus, and the sun. Their religion reflected a deep reverence for natural cycles and the heavens. However, Solomon, as a prophet and king guided by divine authority, sought to redirect the queen and her people from these Pagan rituals toward monotheism and submission to the one true God.

This moment in scripture reveals a theological shift and a power dynamic rooted in prophetic responsibility. Solomon didn't forcefully conquer Sheba—he engaged her mind and spirit. The queen, known for her intellect and authority, recognized the truth in his words and ultimately aligned herself with Solomon's God.

This encounter echoes broader patterns found in history: moments when spiritual accountability challenged empire, and leaders were faced with the decision to uphold ancestral traditions or align with divine justice. In the context of systemic oppression and whitewashed narratives, the Queen of Sheba's story reminds us that wisdom, diplomacy, and transformation once radiated from African kingdoms long before the rise of European dominance.

The bird, who was not long in coming, said: "I have just seen what you know nothing of. With truthful news, I come to you from Sheba, where I found a woman reigning over a people. She is possessed of every virtue and has a splendid throne. I found that she and her subjects worship the sun instead of God. Satan has seduced them and debarred them from the right path, so that they might not be guided to the worship of God, who brings to light all that is concealed in the geographical realm of the Kushites.

The Aryan Caste System (Varna)

The heavens and the earth and know what you hide and what you reveal, God; there is no god but Him, the Lord of the Glorious Throne!" (The Ant 27:22)

The Sabeans of Ethiopia remain shrouded in mystery, but at the heart of their story lies a powerful truth: their rise and fall depended on how faithfully they served the one true God, Yahweh.

The Kushites, Egyptians, and Israelites trace their roots to this ancient civilization. They shared bloodlines and language, likely speaking early forms of Hebrew, the sacred tongue of covenant and prophecy.

For a time, these nations walked in alignment with divine purpose. But their northern neighbors introduced Paganism and false gods. When the Covenant nations—Kush, Egypt, and Israel—embraced the idols of the Aryans, they fell from grace. Their spiritual betrayal led to political downfall, instability, and the loss of divine protection.

The Bible makes these ancestral connections clear. In Isaiah 45:14, Kush, Egypt, and the Sabeans are mentioned together as a unified people of value and purpose. The Israelites, often seen as spiritually unique, are even described elsewhere as the "children of the Kushites," suggesting a shared origin and destiny.

Yet history has tried to erase this lineage. The myth of white spiritual supremacy depends on disconnecting Black and Brown people from their sacred past. But the truth remains: before European empires and colonization, there were Covenant nations—mighty, melanated, and chosen.

Ask Me of things to come concerning My Sons, and the work of My hands. The Labor of Egypt and merchandise of Cush and the Sabeans, men of stature, shall come over in chains; and they shall bow down to you. (Isaiah 45:14)

Because you have set your heart as the heart of a god, Behold, therefore, I will bring strangers against you, the most terrible of the nations; and they shall draw their swords against the beauty of your wisdom, and defile your splendor. They shall throw you down into the Pit, and you shall die the death of the slain amid the seas. (Ezekiel 28:6-29:1)

The Aryans were a nomadic, warlike people who once roamed the regions stretching from the Ganges Valley to the Caucasus Mountains. Though often associated with India and Europe, their ancestral roots can be traced back to ancient Babylon. Many generations after leaving, they returned with vengeance, bringing conquest, cultural disruption, and spiritual confusion.

Described as muscular, long-haired, and light-skinned, the Aryans had distinctly European features. For centuries, they migrated along the Oxus and Jaxartes Rivers, and around the Black and Caspian Seas, eventually pushing into the Indian subcontinent.

Another wave of Aryans—later known as the Hyksos—moved toward the Middle East, settling in regions like Persia, Assyria, Egypt, and Canaan. These groups relentlessly searched for territory, often destabilizing ancient civilizations that had once been aligned with divine covenants.

The Aryans practiced a polytheistic and henotheistic belief system—worshiping multiple gods, each associated with different aspects of nature and cosmic power. Their rituals were centered around appeasing elemental forces and invoking spirits from four realms: the earth, the underworld, the air between, and the lower heavens.

Wherever they went, the Aryans adapted to local deities, aligning themselves with whichever spirits appeared most powerful or useful. Their spiritual system, rooted in domination rather than obedience to a single Creator, stood in stark contrast to the monotheism of the Covenant nations.

Their arrival signaled not just military invasion but also spiritual corruption. The spread of Aryan ideology—rooted in hierarchy, conquest, and polytheism—marked the beginning of caste systems, racial divisions, and imperial religions designed to control rather than liberate.

The Aryans established a rigid social system called Varna, which means "class" or "color." This structure wasn't just about social order but racial superiority. The Aryans believed they came from a divine bloodline with the moral right to rule over all humanity. They called themselves Arya, meaning "noble ones," but the Bible identifies them as Gentiles—foreign to the

Covenant and disconnected from the worship of the one true God, Yahweh.

Driven by pride, arrogance, and a false sense of divine authority, the Aryans spread their ideology across every region they touched. In India, they found a society that had largely turned away from Yahweh. There, they institutionalized their beliefs into the caste system, which outlawed interracial marriage, oppressed indigenous populations, and enforced strict racial and social divisions.

This system of spiritual and social apartheid became a model of domination. Wherever the Aryans expanded, they carried this diabolical order with them. Over time, they became the ancestors of powerful empires: the Assyrian-Babylonians, Greeks, Persians, Romans, Germans, Dutch, Portuguese, Spanish, French, British, and Russians. These nations, rooted in Aryan lineage, formed what the Book of Daniel describes as the "Four Beasts" empires, Gentile world powers that ruled through oppression, exploitation, and racial hierarchy.

Around 1800 B.C., the Aryans began a violent campaign to conquer India's rivers and fertile lands. The native people who resisted, known as the Shudra, Dasa, and Dravidians, were dark-skinned, thick-lipped, and culturally rich, much like the Kushites of Africa. These early inhabitants built strong city fortifications, lived in homes made from baked clay bricks, and kept livestock. However, the Aryans dismissed them as inferior, branding them with derogatory terms and forcing them into the lowest caste—a form of spiritual and social death.

The caste system was not just about class; it was a sacred expression of white supremacy. Furthermore, from it grew the ideological roots of global colonization, racism, and the dehumanization of darker-skinned people—a system that still echoes in today's world of systemic injustice.

The Aryans advanced their conquest through treacherous mountain paths, armed with horse-drawn chariots and advanced weapons unfamiliar to the native inhabitants. With brutal efficiency, they overran the Shudra fortresses, leaving behind a trail of death and devastation. It was one of the earliest—and bloodiest—massacres recorded in human history.

Their primary weapon was the swift and deadly war chariot, which gave them unmatched speed on the battlefield. For long-range attacks, they used the bow; for close combat, they wielded slings, spears, sheaths, and double-edged swords. War was not just a necessity—it was their culture. The Aryans were hardened fighters, skilled in both horseback and chariot warfare.

As they stormed through the land, they pillaged cities, cleared forests, and wiped-out entire communities in a violent crusade for dominance. Their nomadic roots meant they did not know farming or animal husbandry—they relied instead on raiding and scavenging. Unlike the indigenous people, who lived in stable, agrarian societies, the Aryans brought with them destruction, not cultivation.

Once they seized control, the Aryans declared themselves kings and lords over the land. But they soon realized they needed the labor of the people they had conquered. Instead of exterminating all their captives, they enslaved them, forcing them to till the soil, herd livestock, and build their new society under a rigid caste structure designed to keep the conquered in perpetual subjugation.

As they expanded, the Aryans encountered another powerful group of dark-skinned people: the Panis. These people possessed greater wealth and influence than those the Aryans had previously subdued, but the Aryans were unable to conquer them outright. For years, the Panis resisted, retreating into mountainous terrain and launching raids to disrupt Aryan control, often stealing livestock and cutting off food supplies.

But over time, even the Panis were worn down—not by war but by adaptation. Gradually, they began to adopt Aryan customs, and with that came the erosion of their native identities. The Aryan system didn't just conquer people—it absorbed them, restructured them, and erased their memories.

This legacy of violent domination and social engineering set the stage for future systems of enslavement, colonization, and racial caste. The roots of today's global hierarchies can be traced back to this ancient struggle: a campaign of death that evolved into a doctrine of supremacy.

As the Aryans tightened their grip on the land, many of the Shudra and Dasa, once free peoples, were enslaved or driven deep into the forests. Facing an unstoppable force, they chose exile over submission. Rather than cling to dreams of reclaiming their homelands, they became fugitives, forced to flee from an invading system that had declared itself righteous and supreme. To the newly arrived white conquerors, domination wasn't just military—it was justice, carved in stone by a belief in their divine right to rule.

These displaced people—dark-skinned, indigenous, and spiritually rooted—were pushed to the edges of society, both literally and figuratively. Their freedom to live, roam, and worship was stripped away by an invincible caste regime that defined humanity by color, bloodline, and obedience to the Aryan order.

However, not all resisted with weapons. Some, like the Panis, attempted a different form of rebellion: remembrance. The sacred texts of the Vedas—often interpreted through the lens of Aryan dominance—echo a different truth. The Panis, keepers of ancestral knowledge, tried to call the Aryans back from their origin of idolatry. They reminded them of their shared origins, kinship, and former connection to the one true God.

It was a plea for spiritual accountability, a warning against the worship of countless gods crafted in man's image. The Panis knew that what the Aryans had abandoned was not just monotheism but covenant. In turning their backs on that divine relationship, the Aryans had not only corrupted themselves but also unleashed a legacy of violence that would echo across continents and centuries.

Panis: We have hidden the treasure in a place surrounded by mountains. There are cows, horses, and many other riches... we know that you have been frightened by the gods and forced to come here. We look upon you as our sister. Do not return to Indra. O beautiful one! Stay here. We will give you a share of the cows.

Aryans: I cannot be your sister, and you are not my brothers. I do not know these relationships. I only know Indra and the powerful Angirasa. When I return and tell Indra what has happened, he will invade you...O Panis, flee away. (Debroy, 1994)

To solidify their rule, the Aryans created a rigid caste system known as Varna, a Sanskrit term meaning "color" or "class." This social order was designed to maintain strict racial boundaries and prevent any form of interracial mixing. Marriage across caste lines was strictly forbidden. The goal was clear: preserve Aryan bloodlines and suppress the darker-skinned native populations.

The caste system deliberately kept the indigenous Shudra, Dasa, and Dravidian people illiterate and excluded them from all religious services and spiritual rites. They were denied access to temples, sacred texts, and the very concept of divine connection. This system was not just about social hierarchy—it was a racial regime of exclusion, humiliation, and violence.

Every Aryan clan was led by a ruling chief who maintained a private army for tribal defense and domination. These leaders were supported by priests who served as spiritual enforcers, offering sacrifices and rituals to a pantheon of gods believed to control every aspect of life. The priests sought divine approval for conquests and justified brutality as a sacred duty.

Justice and Oppression in the Aryan Varna Caste System

Justice in this system was administered not through fairness but through fear, spiritual coercion, and unseen powers invoked by the priesthood. The Varna system defined every person's worth at birth and locked them into a life of predetermined suffering or privilege until death. Social mobility was impossible, and violations of caste boundaries were met with unspeakable punishments, including mutilation or death.

This racial hierarchy marked one of the darkest chapters in human history. The treatment of the Shudra, Dasa, and Dravidians—beaten, enslaved, skinned alive, and stripped of humanity—was nothing short of genocidal.

At the top of this oppressive system stood the Brahmins— the priestly caste. These men were the self-declared interpreters of the gods and wielded absolute power in Hindu society. They inherited the gods' names and demanded submission from the lower castes and the people they claimed to represent. In their hands, religion became a weapon—used not to liberate souls, but to reinforce the chains of caste, color, and colonial order.

Below the priestly Brahmins in the Aryan-imposed caste system stood the Kshatriya—the rulers and warriors who enforced Aryan dominance through violence and governance. Third were the Vaisyas, mainly composed of commoners and merchants. Many were of mixed Aryan and Dasa ancestry— Aryo-Dasa—a fusion that marked their place in society as applicable but not pure.

Near the bottom of the hierarchy were the Shudra, a class of enslaved or peasant peoples who were reduced to permanent servitude. However, even below them existed an unspoken, brutal truth: the Untouchables. These were the blackest of the native peoples, so dark-skinned that they were deemed too impure to even belong within the caste structure itself.

The Untouchables were spiritual outcasts—excluded from religious life, stripped of rights, and treated as subhuman. Their dark melanin was seen as a curse, a visible sign of divine punishment in the minds of the Aryan elite. Despite their suffering, the Shudra were subconsciously ranked just above them, occupying a social position barely above the floor of society, but still within the structure. The Untouchables, however, were entirely pushed outside of it.

In Hindu society, this invisible yet all-controlling caste system governed every aspect of life—political power, economic opportunity, spiritual participation, and social mobility. A person's caste was fixed at birth and enforced until death. Physical appearance—especially skin tone—became the dominant marker of caste identity and hereditary worth.

Over time, the castes hardened into permanent categories. Melanin became the metric of human value. The darker the skin, the lower the worth. These visual traits were not just social markers—they were encoded into religious law and treated as moral truths. A person's features determine how they live and whether they are considered worthy of dignity, divinity, or even life itself.

This system of racial caste, rooted in Aryan conquest, laid the foundation for colorism, colonization, and white supremacy across the globe. What began in the hills and plains of ancient India would echo through centuries, shaping the brutal hierarchies of empires, slavery, apartheid, and modern racial injustice.

The Indo-Europeans—known today as the Aryans—composed their sacred texts, called the Vedas. There were four in total: the Rig-Veda, Yajur-Veda, Sama-Veda, and Atharva-Veda. These texts were designed to offer prayers, hymns, devotions, and ritual instructions dedicated to a vast array of spiritual beings, many of whom were not gods in the biblical sense, but rather fallen celestial powers.

CHAPTER 3

Aryan Religious Control and Spiritual Domination

The teachings of the Vedas were tightly controlled. Merely overhearing them could lead to death. Punishments were brutal: a person's tongue might be cut out for speaking the Vedas without permission, and their eyes gouged out for seeing the sacred texts. These violent prohibitions were rooted in a more profound truth—the Aryans did not want their religious secrets falling into the hands of the dark-skinned populations they had conquered. Melanin, in their eyes, disqualified one from sacred knowledge.

The Aryan system was centered entirely on ritual, strict sacrifices, and ceremonies to appease their pantheon of deities. There were hundreds of gods—manifestations of nature, war, fertility, and cosmic forces. These were not loving or moral gods but vengeful, transactional, and often violent beings. Chief among them during warfare was Indra, the thunder god of war and storms.

According to the Rig-Veda—the oldest of the Vedas—Indra was portrayed as a divine warrior who despised the dark-skinned Natives for refusing to worship the Aryan gods. In battle, Indra was believed to unleash floods and fire upon Aryan enemies. He became the spiritual symbol of the Aryan conquest, vengeance, and superiority, building what felt like an invisible spiritual wall between whiteness and blackness. The very name India is said to bear the tribal legacy of this god.

Aryan religious ceremonies were elaborate and steeped in mysticism. A vacant seat was often left near the sacred fire for unseen divine guests. The guru, or altar-builder, prepared the offerings and administered mantras—magical chants meant to invoke supernatural forces. Central to these rituals was Soma, a potent hallucinogenic drink made from a mysterious plant. Soma was believed to open a gateway between the physical and spiritual realms, allowing communication with the celestial beings who fed on sacrifice.

These ceremonies reinforced a system where divine favor was reserved for the conquerors, and spiritual exclusion became another form of racialized oppression. Rituals and festivals were not just about communion with the divine; they were tools for maintaining caste, dominance, and the illusion of divine right over the Indigenous populations.

The Soma—a sacred, hallucinogenic drink—was diluted with water, milk, and honey and carefully placed on the grass, often beneath or near an evergreen tree. The evergreen tree held deep spiritual significance for the Aryans. It symbolized life, wealth, and health, and was believed to channel spiritual energy from the spirit world beyond the horizon. The trees were venerated as sacred living altars.

To the Aryans, evergreen trees were not just symbols of vitality but portals to the divine. The whisper of wind through their branches was thought to carry the voices of celestial spirits, and the trees were believed to draw lightning from the heavens, making them natural beacons for communion with the gods.

However, beneath this reverence lay something far darker. The groves of evergreen trees became sacred sites for ritual sacrifice, including, in some of the most horrific accounts, child sacrifice. Newborn infants were considered the highest form of offering; a tragic corruption of spiritual devotion masked in ritualistic glory.

Aryan Sacrificial System and Core Deities

During these ceremonies, the Aryans gave thanks to Indra, their god of storms and war, for destroying rival spiritual powers and annihilating the dark-skinned native peoples. Their sacrificial system centered around three primary deities:

Agni, the fire god, acted as the mouth of all the gods during sacrifice, bridging the human and divine realms. Varuna, the god of the vast, high-arched sky. Indra, the militant thunder god, controller of rain, lightning, and warfare.

These three were the focal point of Aryan worship, representing control over the elements and dominance over all who opposed them. Nevertheless, behind these violent, nature-bound gods stood a deeper, more mysterious figure: Brahma, not to be confused with the Brahmin priesthood.

Brahma was seen as the supreme divine force, more powerful than Indra, Agni, or Varuna. He was all-powerful and all-knowing and understood to be the source from which all creation, both fallen and divine, originated. Brahma was associated with the One, the eternal spiritual reality transcending all material forms.

Brahma was ironically connected to the older spiritual traditions of the Shudra, Dasa, and Panis—those that the Aryans sought to erase. However, to the Aryans, Brahma had become too distant, too abstract. They moved away from worshipping this unseeable, imageless Creator and embraced the more immediate power of elemental gods, rooted in war, fire, and conquest.

In his groundbreaking work The Two Babylons, Reverend Alexander Hislop quotes a passage from the Vedas about Brahma:

"Of Him whose Glory is so great, there is no image... He illumines all, delights all, whence all proceeded; that by which all live when born, and that to which all must return."

This ancient reverence for an invisible, omnipresent Creator stands in stark contrast to the Aryan obsession with ritual sacrifice and racial domination. It reveals a more profound spiritual truth that predated their violent rise and calls us to remember the sacred wisdom that once guided the forgotten peoples of the Earth.

Over time, the Greeks would place Brahma—the all-powerful Creator—among their pantheon of "unknown gods," acknowledging His presence while failing to understand

His essence. Ironically, among the Aryan people, Brahma remained the least worshipped. Despite being the origin of all things, He was too abstract, invisible, and morally demanding for a culture that favored gods of war, vengeance, and material power.

As Aryan tribes migrated and expanded, they merged with the religious systems of the Indus Valley and the Assyro-Babylonians. Though the names of their gods varied, their functions and belief systems were nearly identical. Out of this fusion emerged a complex religious structure—what we now recognize as Hinduism—layered with mythology, ritual, and caste. However, to the Aryans, their gods were no myth. They crafted images, built temples, and worshipped idols with full belief in their divine authority.

One faction of the Aryans invaded the fertile crescent between the Tigris and Euphrates Rivers—later known as Mesopotamia. These invaders evolved into the Assyrians, among human history's most feared and ruthless empires. Splitting off from the hills of Europe and descending into the Middle East, these Aryan tribes became infamous for their unmatched brutality and unrelenting thirst for domination.

Terror marked their warfare. They beheaded and skinned their enemies, hanging scalps in honor of their victories. Women and children were burned alive, crops destroyed, and cities reduced to ruins. Burial pits were filled with the bodies of their victims. They drank blood from enemy skulls and fashioned garments and furniture from human skin. These were not just acts of war—they were rituals of fear designed to dehumanize and dominate.

The Assyrian (Aryans) were merciless and proud. They believed their gods had chosen them to rule, and they viewed dark-skinned peoples as cursed, inferior, and disposable. The depth of their racial hatred ran through every campaign, every conquest, and every religious ritual. In their minds, spiritual favor was tied to whiteness and domination.

They prayed to their gods—not for righteousness or wisdom—but for material gain, land, gold, and victory. They made treaties only when weakened and broke them the moment they regained power. Their morality was solid, based on strength and self-interest. What they could not conquer through warfare, they destroyed through betrayal.

This era of Aryan-Assyrian expansion marked a shift in world history—a brutal transformation of religion into empire, faith into fear, and gods into weapons of domination. The echoes of their cruelty would lay the groundwork for future empires, colonialism, racial hierarchies, and systemic oppression still present today.

After carving a path of terror across Mesopotamia and South Asia, the nomadic Aryans turned their attention toward Africa, specifically Egypt. Until this era, Egypt had remained relatively untouched by foreign invaders. The region—including Ethiopia, Nubia, and Egypt—was united under one monarch, ruling from Memphis. These lands formed the great Kushite Empire, a unified civilization bound by shared culture, language, and religious belief.

Unlike other ancient kingdoms, the Kushite-Egyptian domain did not need city walls or standing armies. It was surrounded by allies, not enemies. Its society was stable, advanced, and spiritually grounded.

The Kushites and Egyptians had already developed writing systems, mathematics, astronomy, and science centuries before their Aryan invaders even settled. Their medical expertise was unmatched. They practiced delicate surgeries, treated open wounds and internal diseases, and were the first known people to set broken bones using cast molds. They pioneered the art of embalming and mummification, preserving the dead with a spiritual reverence that awed even foreign historians.

The Greek historian Herodotus once observed the Ethiopian embalming process and wrote:

"They covered their dead with gypsum, and adorn it with painting until it is as like the living man as possible... then they place the body in a coffin made of crystal pillar which the corpse neither gives out any unpleasant odors."

(Herodotus, 1982)

The Kushite Empire was also a hub of technological and artistic innovation. They developed complex irrigation systems, dams, bridges, and were among the first to build ships and craft glass. Their architecture, sculpting, and monuments reflected spiritual depth and engineering mastery. Their hieroglyphic writing system, etched in stone and painted on papyrus, combined logographic and alphabetic elements, becoming the foundation of religious and historical literature.

While other civilizations wrote on clay tablets or animal skins, the Egyptians and Ethiopians used papyrus—thin, flexible sheets made from the papyrus plant—an early forerunner to modern paper.

Despite these achievements, Egypt faced a catastrophic crisis with the arrival of the Aryans. The peaceful, independent Egyptian kingdom, accustomed to internal tribal skirmishes, was unprepared for an invasion of this magnitude. The Aryans arrived with advanced weaponry and swift horse-drawn chariots, overwhelming a society not structured for war.

Seizing the opportunity, the Aryans pushed deep into Egypt. They extended their conquest down the Nile and into Canaan (modern-day Israel), taking territory from the Hittites and other indigenous peoples.

This marked the beginning of a violent transformation. A civilization built on healing, harmony, and enlightenment fell under the control of an empire built on war, supremacy, and spiritual distortion.

In the early stages of Aryan expansion into Kushite territory, the native rulers chose not to confront the invaders. Instead, they recognized them as foreign rulers and gave them the title Hyksos, meaning "foreign kings." At first, there was a truce. The newcomers brought new technologies and tactics that altered the region's balance of power. With this uneasy peace, Kushite leaders allowed the Hyksos to settle.

However, their attitude changed as the Hyksos' population grew and their clans expanded. What began as coexistence soon shifted into militarism. The once-peaceful settlers became warlike, and corporal punishment became their tool for enforcing submission. Disobedience was met with brutality, and order was maintained through fear.

In many ways, these Balkan settlers reshaped Egypt's reliance on Kush by introducing new forms of warfare. Most notably, they brought the fast-moving horse-drawn chariot and the powerful composite bow—transformative military tools that allowed for long-range attacks and swift battlefield maneuvers. These innovations gave the Hyksos a strategic advantage and forever changed the nature of conflict in the region.

The fragile peace between Kush and Egypt began to fracture. Once unified under a shared cultural and religious foundation, the land was now divided. The Hyksos waged war on Upper Egypt while enslaving the native Egyptians in the Lower Nile Valley. The Egyptians—once proud rulers of a powerful civilization—were demoted to the lowest rung of a newly imported Eurocentric caste system, forced into servitude by foreign occupiers.

Clans from the Balkans continued migrating into Egypt, lured by the promise of free land, valuables, and status. This mass influx shifted the power dynamic further, as the settlers strengthened their hold and expanded their reach. They marched as far as Canaan (modern-day Israel and Palestine), where they established five kingdoms to dominate the trade routes and control the economic lifelines of the region.

The ruling system they installed mirrored that of the Indo-European Aryans in India. At the top stood the pharaoh—a king portrayed as a living god. Surrounding him were nobles and priests, the religious-political elite who oversaw the rituals of domination and divine submission. Below them were the darker-skinned natives—enslaved, exploited, and dehumanized.

The Hyksos did not engage in widespread massacres like their Aryan kin elsewhere, but only because submission brought more utility. So long as the Egyptians bowed their heads, accepted their inferior status, and served the upper class without resistance, they were allowed to live. However, even that life was one of bondage, where power, land, and divine favor were now the property of foreign rulers who had declared themselves gods on Earth.

This moment marked the collapse of an era, when Kush and Egypt no longer stood as unified Black civilizations, but as divided territories under foreign control, spiritual manipulation, and racial caste. Moreover, the echoes of that division would ripple across centuries, influencing how empire, hierarchy, and white supremacy would unfold across the globe.

As the Aryans solidified their rule in Egypt, they imposed their idolatrous system of worship upon the people they had conquered. The upper class, composed of Aryan settlers, seized control of the government, while the native Egyptians were reduced to forced laborers. Temples dedicated to traditional deities were torn down, and new ones were constructed in honor of Aryan gods—representatives of their polytheistic, war-centered belief system.

This religious shift was not just about theology—it was about control. Through the destruction of indigenous spiritual centers and the imposition of foreign gods, the Aryans rewrote the sacred landscape, replacing native connection with subjugation.

During this period of invasion and oppression, many Israelites were caught in bondage alongside the native Egyptians. The Aryans made no distinction between them. Both groups were dark-skinned, and to the conquerors, melanin was the marker of inferiority. The Israelites suffered the same harsh treatment as the Egyptians under the emerging Eurocentric caste structure.

The biblical story of Joseph illustrates this crossover in history. Sold into slavery by his brothers, Joseph was taken to Egypt and placed under Potiphar, an officer of Pharaoh's court (Genesis 37:17). This brought Joseph into the heart of Egyptian society, where he eventually rose to the position of prime minister (Vizier), second only to Pharaoh. This story is set in the city of Dothan, west of the Jordan River and northeast of Samaria.

A severe drought in Canaan later caused Jacob and his family to migrate southward, seeking refuge in Egypt. In his position of authority, Joseph granted his family permission to settle in Goshen (Wadi Tumilat), near the eastern Nile Delta. Scholars place Joseph's entry into Egypt around 1900–1850 B.C., likely during the 12th Dynasty of Egypt, when the land was still under Ethiopian-Kushite rule and before Aryan control had fully taken root.

Significantly, Aryan occupation and systemic oppression appear to have intensified after Joseph's time. The rise of the Hyksos—Aryan-linked foreigners—would later bring about a new era of bondage. The prophet Isaiah saw clearly that the Hyksos and the Assyrians, despite their geographic separation, were one people culturally and spiritually. In his writings, Isaiah describes the brutal conditions of Israelite enslavement under foreign powers—conditions that mirror the racialized violence and forced labor imposed by the Aryan invaders.

The story of Joseph, Goshen, and the shifting political climate reminds us that the Israelites and Egyptians once coexisted in a shared struggle under foreign domination. Isaiah's prophecy traces a connection from the Aryan conquests to the rise of global systems built on caste hierarchies—structures that still influence our world today.

For thus says the Lord God:

My people went down at first into Egypt to dwell there; then the Assyrian oppressed them without cause. Now therefore, what have I here," says the Lord, "That My people are taken away for nothing? Those who rule over them make them wail," says the Lord.

(Isaiah 52:44-45)

The Aryans likely invaded Egypt around a century after Joseph's death, gradually consolidating power through the Hyksos dynasty. Their reign endured until the late 1500s B.C., when their oppressive rule came to an end during Egypt's Eighteenth Dynasty under King Ahmose I. During this time, the native Egyptians, especially those in Lower Egypt, rose with the strategic support of the Kushites from the south. Together, they launched a successful campaign to reclaim control of the Nile Delta, forcing the Aryans into retreat.

However, once the Aryans were expelled, unity was short-lived. The Kushites, who had long regarded Egypt as part of their cultural and political domain, sought to reclaim authority over the now-divided territory. These competing claims led to prolonged regional tensions and border skirmishes, which persisted even into the time of Moses.

By the time Moses came of age during the Eighteenth Dynasty, Egypt had regained much of its independence and military strength. Moses, raised in Pharaoh's household, was recognized for his brilliance and leadership. The king summoned him to command the Egyptian army in battle, and under Moses's direction, Egypt achieved significant military victories.

His success, however, sparked jealousy within the royal court. His rising influence and charisma were seen as a threat to the elites, and plots to assassinate him began to circulate.

The Jewish historian Josephus recounts a war during the reign of Thutmose I, in which the Egyptians faced the Ethiopians—likely a remnant conflict involving Kushite military power. It is believed that Thutmose's military campaigns laid the foundation for Egypt's rise as the world's first superpower, uniting advanced warfare with political expansion.

Following Thutmose's reign, Egypt experienced a cultural and artistic transformation. The Cretans' migration out of the Aegean brought the elegant and dynamic artistic style of the Minoans to Egypt, ushering in a new era of creative expression.

However, Egypt's spiritual transformation came under the radical Pharaoh Amenhotep IV, later known as Akhenaten, who sought to abandon polytheism and center religious life around one deity—Aten. After Akhenaten's death, religious power structures shifted again, and the political climate grew unstable.

It was in this climate that Prince Moses, now an outcast, fled Egypt through the desert to Midian. There, among the descendants of the Ethiopians, he found refuge, favor, and ultimately, his divine calling.

This moment marks a pivotal transition—from empire and oppression to liberation and prophetic purpose. Moses's life bridges two worlds: the oppressive Aryan-Egyptian system built on caste, war, and idolatry, and the covenantal order of justice, freedom, and divine sovereignty that would define the next chapter in the story of the Israelites and the legacy of the Kushite-Egyptian struggle.

For more than a century after the Aryans were expelled, the Israelites continued to enjoy the privileges granted to them through Joseph's legacy. Though the Aryan rulers had been cast out, their influence lingered. Egypt had absorbed its governing style, caste-based social order, military campaigns, and even gods. The spiritual and political systems of the Aryans remained deeply embedded in Egyptian society.

In the process, the Egyptians lost touch with the Creator—Yahweh, the true God. The memory of divine covenant faded as the people embraced a pantheon of Aryanized deities and a hierarchy built on bloodline and race.

Meanwhile, the Israelites lived quietly among the Egyptians. Though it was rumored they were a chosen people—favored by a God so holy that even the divine beings of other realms would bow in His presence—their way of life did not yet reflect this spiritual inheritance. They had grown comfortable in Egypt, a land of power, prosperity, and prestige—an earthly paradise that seemed invincible.

However, as time passed, Egypt fully embraced the gods of its former invaders. During the New Kingdom, the Egyptians adopted many Aryan deities and merged them with their own. Chief among them was Amun-Ra, a composite figure who became king of the gods. Grand temples were erected in his honor, and pyramids throughout Nubia bore witness to his worship. Amun's influence extended beyond spiritual life—he became a symbol of imperial conquest and divine kingship.

Egypt's military victories were increasingly credited to the hidden power of Zeus-Amun, a syncretized god that reflected the fusion of Indo-European and African religious ideologies. His oracle, located at the border of Egypt and Ethiopia, became a sacred site visited by kings seeking divine favor, including Alexander the Great, during his famed campaigns.

Nevertheless, for the Israelites, the golden era was ending. Their noble status faded. Their connection to the throne, once preserved through Joseph, was now forgotten. The Bible marks this turning point clearly:

"Now there arose a new king over Egypt who did not know Joseph."

(Exodus 1:8)

This new regime no longer viewed the Israelites as allies, but as a threat—foreigners multiplying within their borders. The Aryanized Egyptian elite saw them not as the children of the covenant, but as expendable labor. And so began the long descent into bondage.

Moses' Divine Encounter

After 40 years in exile, having fled Egypt as a fugitive, Moses was tending the flock of his father-in-law, Jethro, in the land of Midian. During this quiet chapter of his life, Moses encountered something extraordinary. On the slopes of Mount Sinai, he saw a bush engulfed in flame—yet not consumed by it. As he turned aside to witness the mystery, the presence of God met him.

Then the voice called out:

"Moses, Moses!" And Moses answered, "Here I am." The Lord said, "Do not draw near this place. Take your sandals off your feet, for where you stand is holy ground. I am the God of your father—the God of Abraham, the God of Isaac, and the God of Jacob."

Overwhelmed by the presence of the Creator, Moses hid his face in fear.

And the Lord continued:

"I have surely seen the oppression of My people who are in Egypt, and have heard their cry because of their taskmasters, for I know their sorrow."

This was the turning point—not just for Moses, but for an entire nation. The same God whose name had been forgotten under the weight of Aryan gods, empire, and idol worship was now calling His people back. Yahweh had not forgotten His covenant. He had heard the cries of the oppressed. And through Moses, He would begin the great work of liberation— breaking the chains of the empire and restoring the dignity of a people long buried under bricks and burdens.

Moses returned to Egypt—not as a fugitive, but as a divine messenger, charged with confronting the most powerful ruler in the known world. He came with one demand, spoken not in his name, but in the name of the Creator:

"Let My people go, that they may hold a feast to Me in the wilderness."

Pharaoh, hardened by pride and empire, scoffed at the command.

"Who is the Lord that I should obey His voice to let Israel go? I do not know the Lord, nor will I let Israel go."

This was not merely a political rejection—it was a spiritual rebellion. Pharaoh defied the Creator Himself, refusing to release a people marked by covenant, descendants of Abraham, Isaac, and Jacob. What followed was not just a battle of wills, but a divine confrontation between Yahweh and the false gods of the empire.

At the beginning of Exodus chapter 7, God speaks directly to Moses:

"See, I have made you as God to Pharaoh, and Aaron your brother shall be your prophet... I will harden Pharaoh's heart and multiply My signs and My wonders in the land of Egypt. But Pharaoh will not heed you, so that I may lay My hand on Egypt and bring My armies and My people-the children of Israel—out of the land of Egypt by great judgments."

What unfolded next were the plagues—ten acts of divine justice that dismantled Egypt's spiritual, agricultural, and political systems. Yahweh exposed Pharaoh's false power and brought judgment against every god in the Egyptian pantheon. The land that had once enslaved the covenant people would now witness their deliverance by the hand of the true God.

Three months after the Israelites escaped Egypt and crossed the Red Sea, they arrived at Mount Sinai. There, the Lord descended upon the mountain in power, enveloped in a thick cloud, with fire, smoke, and the blast of a trumpet so loud the people trembled. This was not myth or ritual—it was a divine encounter.

On that mountain, God's covenant with Abraham, Isaac, and Jacob was confirmed to their descendants. It was not only a legal agreement—it was an identity. It separated the Israelites from the idolatrous and pagan nations that surrounded them. It reestablished their purpose: to be a holy people, chosen to walk in justice, mercy, and truth.

This covenant became the dividing line between loyalty to an empire, obedience, spiritual truth, and religious domination. The children of Israel were no longer just freed slaves—they were a covenant nation, called out from the systems that uplifted them through supremacy, caste, and idolatry to become a living witness of the one true God.

During the Israelites' wilderness journey, internal tensions arose. Miriam and Aaron—Moses' siblings—spoke against him for marrying an Ethiopian woman, the daughter of a Kushite king. According to Israelite tradition, marriages were to occur within one's tribe to preserve covenantal lineage. But Moses had taken his wife during his exile in Midian, a province of ancient Kush, and her Ethiopian heritage sparked controversy.

Their criticism, however, provoked an immediate divine response. In the Book of Numbers, it reads:

"And the cloud departed above the tabernacle, and suddenly Miriam became leprous, white as snow. Then Aaron turned toward Miriam, and there she was, a leper. So, Aaron said to Moses, 'Oh, my lord! Please do not lay this sin on us, in which we have done foolishly and in which we have sinned."

(Numbers 12:10-11)

This moment was a profound indictment against ethnic prejudice. God defended Moses and made a public statement: the covenant was not bound by ethnicity alone but by obedience, humility, and divine purpose.

As the Israelites continued their journey, they approached the border of Edom. Moses sent a diplomatic message to the king, requesting safe passage through the land. Camping at Kadesh, Moses appealed to their shared ancestry:

> "Thus says your brother Israel: You know all the hardship that has befallen us... How our fathers went down to Egypt, and the Egyptians afflicted us and our fathers."

But the king of Edom refused. Although Moses called the Edomites "brethren," they allowed envy, fear, and pride to separate them from their kin. Israel was forced to turn away— yet another rejection from a people who once knew Yahweh.

When the Israelites reached Acacia Grove, near Moab, the tensions escalated. Balak, king of Moab, was terrified. Israel had defeated the Amorites and now seemed unstoppable. In desperation, Balak summoned the prophet Balaam to curse the Israelites.

Balaam, though initially hesitant, devised a corrupt strategy: not to curse Israel directly, but to entice them into sin. The Epistle of Jude warns of this very deception:

> *"Woe to them! For they have gone in the way of Cain, have run greedily in the error of Balaam for profit, and perished in the rebellion of Korah."*

(Jude 1:11)

Balaam encouraged the Moabites and Midianites to seduce the Israelites into Baal worship, inviting them to sacrifices and sexual immorality. This idolatrous infiltration angered the Lord, not just because of ritual defilement, but because it threatened to sever Israel's identity as a covenant people, distinct from the surrounding nations.

The tragedy is that Moab, Edom, and Midian were not strangers to Yahweh. These nations had ancestral roots in the knowledge of God, but they had compromised, allowing the idolatry of surrounding cultures to corrupt their worship. Over time, these cultures merged with what became known as the Five Kings of the Philistines—nations that adopted pagan rites and eventually became Israel's fiercest enemies.

CHAPTER 4

Aryan Dominion: Ritual, Empire, and Spiritual Corruption

The Philistines would go on to challenge Israel's destiny for generations. They were eventually defeated in a major naval battle by Rameses III, who drove them from Egypt's coast and pushed them deeper into Syria and southern Canaan at the dawn of the Iron Age.

Nevertheless, the seeds of conflict had already been sown: fear, envy, betrayal, and compromise. The Israelites were not only fighting battles with swords—they were in a spiritual war for their identity, tested by temptation from within and rejection from outsiders.

According to Egyptian records, the Philistines were the final wave of Aryan invaders to challenge Egypt during the Twentieth Dynasty. Their attempt came during the reign of Rameses III, who ruled for 31 years. The Philistines—part of a larger group referred to as the Sea Peoples—launched an aggressive naval campaign but were ultimately repelled by Rameses's forces, marking one of the last successful defenses of Egypt's ancient sovereignty.

But the threat to Egypt didn't end with the Philistines. By the seventh century B.C., a new Aryan power emerged—the Assyrians. Under the leadership of Esarhaddon, the Assyrians marched into Memphis and captured Egypt, marking the beginning of their campaign for global domination. Like their predecessors, they were driven by conquest and religious supremacy, continuing the Aryans legacy of subjugating darker-skinned civilizations.

The origins of the Philistines remain shrouded in mystery, but the Book of Genesis offers a glimpse:

"From whom the Philistines came" (Genesis 10:14)— linking them to two tribal groups: the Pathrusim and Casluhim. These people eventually settled in Caphtor, a coastal region generally identified with the island of Crete (ancient Greece).

The Aryans, having moved into Crete, burned settlements and displaced indigenous cultures. From there, they pushed eastward along the Mediterranean, moving through Syria, the southern coastal plains, and the central highlands of Canaan. The Philistines and Caphtorim formed a seafaring coalition of Aryan origin—fierce, mobile, and materialistic. Their goal was not merely conquest, but the extraction of wealth, land, and spiritual dominance.

Upon entering Canaan (Israel), they targeted three key cities: Gaza, Ashkelon, and Ashdod. These cities became the foundation of Philistine power and culture. With them, they brought their religious system—polytheistic and pagan—featuring gods like Baal, Astarte, and Dagon. These deities represented fertility, war, and elemental forces, and their worship included practices that directly opposed the covenantal standards of Israel.

The Philistines were not just political enemies of Israel—they were spiritual antagonists. Their gods demanded human sacrifice, sexual immorality, and ritual violence, forming a religious system rooted in domination rather than divine justice. Their presence in the land became a constant threat to Israel's identity, purity, and purpose.

As descendants of the Aryan expansion, the Philistines embodied the same pattern seen from the time of the Hyksos and the Assyrians: militarized conquest, cultural erasure, and religious perversion—all aimed at subjugating covenant nations and elevating a racialized, idolatrous order.

Philistine Expansion and Military Advantage

Following their conquest of Gaza, Ashkelon, and Ashdod, the Philistines expanded deeper into the land of Canaan, taking two more strategic coastal cities: Gath and Ekron. These cities, positioned farther inland along the Yarkon River, extended their influence across the tribal territories of Dan and Judah.

The Philistines were not just warriors—they were shrewd and highly organized. Their economy was renowned for its innovation and efficiency. They excelled in tool-making, controlled the production and distribution of alcoholic beverages, and employed cunning trade and military tactics that gave them dominance over surrounding peoples.

One of their greatest advantages was their mastery of ironworking. Unlike the Israelites, who had limited access to this advanced metallurgy, the Philistines possessed superior weapons made of iron and bronze. They also used horse-driven chariots to have devastating effects on the battlefield. Their iron technology fueled their military superiority and became the foundation of a robust economy on which the Israelites increasingly depended.

The Philistines went to great lengths to guard the secrets of iron fabrication, ensuring the Israelites could not rise against them with comparable force. Their rule marked a dark period of subjugation. The Israelites, having turned away from Yahweh, found themselves enslaved by a foreign people, forced to rely on the Philistines for basic survival needs like food, tools, and clothing. The freedom they once enjoyed was replaced with economic dependence and cultural humiliation. But God had not forgotten His people.

Amid oppression, the Lord raised Samson—the last of the Judges—as a deliverer to call Israel back to Himself. Unlike traditional warriors, Samson was born under a Nazarite vow and empowered by the Spirit of God. His strength was legendary, but his mission was divine: to disrupt the Philistine domination and ignite a spark of resistance among his people.

One of the most infamous episodes in Samson's story began with personal tragedy. After escalating tensions, Samson torched the Philistines' grain fields, vineyards, and olive groves. He did this by tying torches to the tails of 300 foxes and releasing them into the Philistine farmlands—crippling their agricultural economy in an act of divine vengeance.

In retaliation, the Philistines descended on Judah and burned Samson's wife and her father alive, hoping to break his will and reassert dominance. But this only deepened Samson's fury and commitment to his God-given purpose.

Samson's life—marked by supernatural strength, personal weakness, and a final act of sacrifice—would stand as both judgment and prophecy. He was a living symbol of God's power to raise deliverance even in the darkest times, and a reminder that no empire, no matter how technologically advanced, could stand forever against divine justice.

The Philistines, determined to destroy their greatest threat, hunted Samson through the Sorek Valley. There, he had fallen in love with a woman named Delilah, a harlot whom the Philistine lords persuaded to seduce him and uncover the secret of his strength.

Driven by lust, emotional vulnerability, and perhaps drunken pride, Samson eventually gave in to her persistent questioning. With humor and arrogance, he concealed the truth for a time, but eventually, he confessed the covenant that defined his entire purpose:

"No razor has ever come upon my head, for I have been a Nazirite to God from my mother's womb. If I am shaven, then my strength will leave me, and I shall become weak, and be like any other man."

(Judges 16:17)

While Samson slept in Delilah's lap, she summoned a man to shave his head. At that moment, the divine strength that once set him apart left him. The Philistines rushed in, overpowered him, and bound him. To humiliate him further, they gouged out his eyes, stripping him not only of strength but also of vision—both literal and symbolic.

Samson was taken in chains to Gaza, the heart of Philistine power. Clothed in bronze fetters, he was forced to grind grain in prison—once a feared warrior, now reduced to a beast. His downfall became a spectacle for his enemies, a triumph for the Philistine over the chosen of God. But Samson's story was not yet finished.

At a grand celebration, the lords of the Philistines gathered in the Temple of Dagon to worship their god and revel in their victory. Over 3,000 men and women—many of them crowded on the rooftop—came to witness Samson's humiliation. They brought him out to perform like a captured animal.

Blinded, broken, and mocked, Samson called upon the God he had once neglected but never stopped belonging to:

"O Lord God, remember me, I pray! Strengthen me, I pray, just this once, O God, that I may with one blow take vengeance on the Philistines for my two eyes!" (Judges 16:28)

Led by a servant boy to the two central pillars supporting the temple, Samson stretched out his arms and pushed with all his might. With one final act of divine strength, he brought the entire structure down upon himself and his enemies.

The Temple of Dagon collapsed, crushing the Philistine elites. Samson died with his enemies, killing more in his death than he had during his life.

This moment was not just vengeance—it was prophetic. It was a declaration that no empire, no god of oppression, and no system built on domination and mockery could stand forever against the will of Yahweh. Samson's death symbolized sacrificial resistance—a foreshadowing of a coming kingdom where true strength would be rooted not in an empire, but in obedience, justice, and spiritual power.

In time, the Israelites gained the upper hand over the Philistines—but not by their strength alone. They found common cause with other Kushite tribes in Canaan who shared a Hebrew dialect and a similar ancestral memory. Among these groups, the Hittites were the largest. Though often regarded as an inferior social class under Philistine rule, these Hebrew-speaking tribes had long resisted foreign domination. Together, they launched guerrilla-style raids on Philistine towns and strongholds.

Under the prophetic leadership of Samuel and the rising authority of Saul, Israel's first king, a coalition formed—not just military, but spiritual. Samuel's call was clear and uncompromising:

"If you return to the Lord with all your hearts, then put away the foreign gods and the Ashtoreth from among you, and serve Him only; and He will deliver you from the hand of the Philistines."

(1 Samuel 7:3)

The Israelites repented and renewed their covenant. In a pivotal battle, the Lord responded with a thunderous sign, confusing the Philistines and delivering them into Israel's hands. The Israelites reclaimed lost territory and tasted victory again. Yet this moment of triumph echoed an earlier warning from the Exodus journey:

"You shall not bow down to their gods, nor serve them, nor do according to their works; but you shall utterly overthrow them and completely break down their sacred pillars. So, you shall serve the Lord your God, and He will bless your bread and your water. And I will take sickness away from the midst of you."

(Exodus 23:24-25)

This covenant command was not just about land—it was about identity. The Israelites were instructed to tear down the false systems of worship, not tolerate them. But instead of entirely driving out the Philistines and dismantling their idols, Israel absorbed elements of their culture, rituals, and religious traditions.

Worse still, theological confusion began to grow within the broader Hebrew-speaking community. Though many of these non-Exodus tribes shared a common tongue, they did not all share the same spiritual allegiance. Some had adopted the Canaanite faith, mixing their belief in Yahweh with the worship of Baal, Ashtoreth, and other regional deities. These discrepancies created tension and division within the broader Hebrew population.

The danger was no longer just external oppression—it was internal compromise. Israel's greatest challenge was no longer the Philistine army, but the erosion of covenant distinctiveness through cultural absorption and religious syncretism.

What began as a call to freedom risked becoming a slow descent into spiritual captivity—a warning that remains relevant to every generation of people called by God's name.

So, the Lord was with Judah. And they drove out the mountaineers, but they could not drive out the inhabitants of the lowland, because they had chariots of iron... However, Manasseh did not drive out the inhabitants of Beth Shean and its villages, or Taanach and its villages... for the Canaanites were determined to dwell in the land. And it came to pass, when Israel was strong, that they put the Canaanites under tribute, but did not completely drive them out. (Judges 1:19-28)

Then the Angel of the Lord came up from Gilgal to Bochim, and said, "I led you up from Egypt and brought you to the land of which I swore to your fathers;" and I said, "I will never break My covenant with you. And you should make no covenant with the inhabitants of this land; you shall tear down their altar." But you have not obeyed My voice. Why have you done this? "Therefore, I also said, 'I will not drive them out before you, but they shall be a thorn in your side, and their gods shall be a snare to you.'" (Judges 2:1-3)

Israel's Coalition and Spiritual Struggles

Ahab, the son of King Omri, was the seventh king of Israel and one of its most prominent and politically gifted rulers. His reign, marked by expansion, infrastructure, and wealth, drew comparisons to that of King Solomon a century earlier. But like Solomon, Ahab's rise to power came with spiritual compromise that would have lasting consequences for Israel.

Solomon introduced Paganism into the nation by marrying foreign wives who brought their gods with them.

Ahab followed a similar path, only with greater intensity. To strengthen his alliance with the Phoenicians, Ahab married Jezebel, the daughter of Ethbaal, king of Tyre, a high priest of Baal. This political marriage was intended to secure peace and trade, but it brought spiritual corruption into the heart of Israel.

To please Jezebel, Ahab permitted—and later promoted—the worship of Baal, erecting altars and allowing sacrifices alongside those dedicated to Yahweh. He also built a wooden image of Asherah, a Canaanite fertility goddess, further defiling the spiritual purity of the land. Jezebel was not merely a foreign queen—she was a militant promoter of Baal worship who actively persecuted Yahweh's prophets and sought to erase true worship from Israel altogether.

Despite his spiritual failures, Ahab was a formidable leader in governance and military strategy. He completed the construction of Samaria, establishing it as Israel's capital and administrative center. He also oversaw rebuilding Hazor, an ancient city with strategic importance in the north.

Hazor became a vital military stronghold, protecting Israel's northern borders. Ahab restored the city and fortified it with walls and defensive structures. Near the southern edge of the mound, a tunnel system was carved to ensure access to a steady water supply in times of siege. His vision extended beyond Hazor—other fortresses were constructed throughout the kingdom to strengthen Israel's national security.

Yet, for all his accomplishments, Ahab's legacy was tainted by his blending political pragmatism with spiritual rebellion. By allowing Baal worship to coexist with the worship of Yahweh, he blurred the lines of covenant identity. His decisions laid the foundation for internal division, prophetic confrontation, and national judgment.

Ahab's story is cautionary, reminding us that prosperity without spiritual integrity leads to collapse. During his reign, the prophet Elijah rose to challenge a king and an entire culture sliding into apostasy.

Under King Ahab's leadership, Israel experienced remarkable financial stability and military advancement. The nation became renowned as the most successful chariot-building power in the region. In Megiddo, Ahab restored the city walls and reinforced its gates, fortifying it as a key defense post. His diplomatic efforts also established peace with Judah, the southern kingdom, momentarily uniting the divided Hebrew peoples under a fragile regional alliance.

But Ahab's reign was not without its fatal flaw. His tragic legacy lay in his deep association with idolatry.

Among the Israelite population was a significant presence of non-Covenant Canaanites—people whom God had explicitly commanded Israel to remove from the land during the pre-Exodus era. Instead of obeying, the Israelites tolerated their presence, absorbed their customs, and began to imitate their religious practices. Shrines were built, and rituals once native to the Philistines and Canaanites became common among the Israelites.

Though Israel flourished economically, Jezebel's influence cast a dark shadow. She was no passive queen; she was an active force of rebellion, embodying what her name and her god, Baal, represented: defiance against the God of Israel. She replaced Yahweh's sanctuaries with altars to Baal and

Asherah, and relentlessly persecuted the prophets and anyone who remained faithful to the Lord.

Ahab, captivated by Jezebel and swayed by her politics, saw no error in blending Israel's covenant faith with paganism. He erected a massive altar to Baal, constructed wooden images of Asherah, and permitted foreign artisans—idol worshipers—to participate in Israel's rebuilding efforts without restriction. Worship of Baal became normalized, and moral corruption followed close behind.

This spiritual decay provoked divine judgment.

The prophet Elijah rose with a voice of righteous defiance and confronted Ahab directly:

"As the Lord God of Israel lives, before whom I stand, there shall not be dew nor rain these years, except at my word."

(1 Kings 17:1)

Elijah's pronouncement of famine wasn't just a punishment—it was a symbolic strike against Baal, who was believed to be the god of storms and fertility. Yahweh demonstrated His unmatched authority by withholding rain and exposing Baal as powerless. It was a confrontation between the God of the Covenant and the gods of cultural compromise.

Ahab's prosperity could not protect him from the consequences of spiritual disobedience. His reign stands as a sobering reminder that material success means nothing when a nation's soul has bowed to false gods.

The prophet Elijah openly criticized Ahab. When Ahab saw Elijah coming, Ahab said, "Is that you, O troublers of Israel?" He answered, "I have not troubled Israel, but you and your father's house have, in that you have forsaken the commandments of the Lord and followed Baal" (1 Kings 18:17-18).

The prophet Elijah, filled with the Spirit of the Lord, issued a bold challenge to King Ahab: summon the 450 prophets of Baal and the 400 priests of Asherah—those who ate at Jezebel's table—to Mount Carmel for a divine contest.

Standing before the wavering people of Israel, Elijah declared:

"How long will you falter between two opinions? If the Lord is God, follow Him; but if Baal, follow him."

(1 Kings 18:21)

The terms were simple but profound. Elijah continued:

"I alone am left a prophet of the Lord, but Baal's prophets are four hundred and fifty men. Let them choose one bull for themselves, cut it into pieces, and lay it on the wood, but put no fire under it. I will do the same. Then you call on the name of your gods, and I will call on the name of the Lord—and the God who answers by fire, He is God."

The people agreed. From morning until noon, the prophets of Baal cried out:

"Baal, hear us!"

They danced, shouted, and cut themselves until blood flowed, but there was no voice, no fire, no answer. Elijah mocked them:

"Cry louder! Maybe your god is meditating, busy, or on a journey—or maybe he's asleep and needs to be awakened!"

Still, silence.

Then Elijah called the people to him. He rebuilt the altar of the Lord, using twelve stones to represent the twelve tribes of Israel. He dug a trench around it and had the people pour water over the sacrifice, three times, until the trench overflowed.

Then Elijah prayed.

"Lord God of Abraham, Isaac, and Israel, let it be known this day that You are God in Israel... Answer me, O Lord, that this people may know You are the Lord God."

Immediately, fire fell from heaven. It consumed the sacrifice, the wood, the stones—even the water in the trench. The people fell on their faces and cried out:

"The Lord, He is God! The Lord, He is God!"

Elijah responded quickly:

"Seize the prophets of Baal! Let not one of them escape!"

They were taken to the Brook Kishon and executed—a decisive judgment against spiritual corruption.

After the victory, Elijah went back to the top of Mount Carmel to pray for rain. Seven times he sent his servant to look toward the sea. On the seventh time, a cloud the size of a man's hand appeared. Soon, the sky turned black, the wind howled, and rain poured down, ending the years-long drought—just as Elijah had prophesied.

But the victory was short-lived in the political realm. When Jezebel heard of what had happened, her fury was unrelenting. She vowed to kill Elijah. The prophet fled to Mount Horeb and found refuge in a cave. There, God spoke to him—not in fire or storm, but in a still, small voice—and commanded him to return and continue his mission.

CHAPTER 5

Judgment and Empire: The Fall of Israel and Judah

Meanwhile, Jezebel's reign of terror continued. She orchestrated the murder of Naboth, an innocent man, simply to seize his vineyard for Ahab. Elijah confronted the king at the scene of the crime. Overwhelmed by guilt, Ahab tore his clothes and sought forgiveness—but judgment was already set in motion.

Ahab later died in battle against Damascus, fulfilling Elijah's prophecy. His son Ahaziah succeeded him but continued in idolatry. Shortly into his reign, Ahaziah fell from the upper balcony of his palace in Samaria. Instead of turning to God, he sent messengers to consult Baal-Zebub, the god of Ekron, about his recovery.

But Elijah intercepted them with a message from the Lord:

"Is it because there is no God in Israel that you are going to inquire of Baal-Zebub, god of Ekron? Therefore, you shall not come down from the bed to which you have gone up, but you shall surely die."

(2 Kings 1:34)

Enraged by Elijah's prophecy, Ahaziah sent two companies of fifty men to arrest him. Both were consumed by fire from heaven. Only when a third captain approached with humility did Elijah give in.

The story of Elijah remains a declaration that God alone rules over kings, prophets, and nations—and that no empire, idol, or Jezebel can stand against the fire of divine truth.

After Ahaziah's death, his brother Jehoram ascended to the throne and ruled Israel for twelve years. Though Jehoram removed the public pillars of Baal, the spiritual decay introduced by his mother Jezebel still poisoned the heart of the nation. Jezebel's influence, rooted in paganism and idolatry, had brought the wrath of God upon Israel, and Jehoram did little to reverse its course.

Jehoram's end came suddenly and with divine irony. As he rode out to meet his military commander Jehu at the vineyard that once belonged to Naboth the Jezreelite—the very property stolen through Jezebel's bloodshed—Jehu struck him down (2 Kings 9:21). It was a moment of judgment exacted on the same ground that cried out for justice.

The prophet Elisha, successor to Elijah, had anointed Jehu as king while Jehoram was still wounded from battle in Ramoth Gilead. Jehu embarked on a brutal, God-ordained purge to wipe out every remnant of Ahab's dynasty. No one was spared—relatives, servants, friends—all connected to Ahab and Jezebel were slain.

Jezebel's death was just as gruesome and symbolic as her reign. Jehu ordered her eunuchs to throw her from a window. Her body was trampled beneath horses, and later, devoured by dogs. Only her skull, hands, and feet remained for burial (2 Kings 9:32-36). Her legacy, like her body, was reduced to fragments—judgment against a woman who sought to erase the name of Yahweh from Israel.

Meanwhile, in the southern kingdom of Judah, another king was leading his people into apostasy—Ahaz, one of the most wicked rulers in Judah's history. During his reign, he sought military protection from Assyria against the threat of Damascus and Israel, who were pressuring him to join an anti-Assyrian alliance. Instead of trusting in God, Ahaz submitted to the empire and paid tribute to Assyria.

In doing so, he welcomed their Pagan culture and brought it directly into Jerusalem's temple. He replaced the altar of the Lord with a replica of a foreign altar from Damascus, desecrating the holy sanctuary. Ahaz embraced the Assyrian gods—Baal, Rimmon, and others—erecting images and burning incense in high places, under evergreen trees, and in secluded valleys.

One of his most abominable acts was the child sacrifice of his sons in the Valley of Hinnom, offered in fire to the god Rimmon. He also practiced witchcraft, sorcery, soothsaying, and consulted evil spirits, plunging Judah into deep spiritual darkness. The prophet Isaiah warned him and pleaded for repentance, but Ahaz hardened his heart.

Ahaz even justified his apostasy with twisted logic:

"Because the gods of the kings of Syria helped them, I will sacrifice to them that they may help me."

(2 Chronicles 28:23)

But the gods of the nation brought no help—only corruption. Ahaz's reign provoked the Lord to anger, and his actions triggered consequences that would lead Judah closer to judgment.

In desperation to secure his throne, King Ahaz stripped treasures from the royal palace and the temple of the Lord to gain favor with Tiglath-Pileser III, king of Assyria. He hoped that an alliance with the Assyrian Empire would protect Judah from the rising threat of Israel and Syria. But the prophet Isaiah warned Ahaz that his political maneuvering would fail and urged him to ask God for a sign instead.

Ahaz, cloaking his rebellion in false humility, refused Isaiah's request, saying:

"I will not ask, nor will I test the Lord."

(Isaiah 7:12)

In truth, Ahaz had already chosen to trust in Assyria rather than in Yahweh. Despite Ahaz's tribute, Assyria did not intervene. Israel and Syria invaded Judah, capturing 200,000 Judeans and plundering their wealth. As the victorious soldiers returned near Samaria, they were confronted by the prophet Oded, who spoke on behalf of the Lord:

"Because the Lord God of your fathers was angry with Judah, He has delivered them into your hand; but you have killed them in a rage that reaches up to heaven. Now you propose to make the children of Judah and Jerusalem your slaves—but are you not also guilty before the Lord your God? Return the captives, for the fierce wrath of the Lord is upon you." (2 Chronicles 28:9–11)

Remarkably, some of the Israelites heeded the prophet. They clothed the captives, fed them, anointed their wounds, and gave them safe passage home—an act of compassion amidst judgment.

Ahaz, however, continued to spiral. Instead of repenting, he doubled down on his idolatry. He looted the Lord's temple again to pay more tribute to Assyria, but the Assyrians still offered no help. The Scriptures record:

"Now in the time of his distress, King Ahaz became increasingly unfaithful to the Lord... For Ahaz took part of the treasures from the house of the Lord... but he did not help him." (2 Chronicles 28:21-22)

The Death of Ahaz and Rise of Hoshea

When Ahaz died, he was buried in Jerusalem—but not in the tombs of the kings. He was denied the honor of a royal burial, a final statement on his disgrace.

Meanwhile, in the Northern Kingdom, Hoshea took the throne in the twelfth year of Ahaz's reign. With Assyrian backing, he assassinated King Pekah and established himself as a puppet ruler. Pekah had refused to continue paying tribute to Assyria in a last-ditch attempt to regain national independence, but his resistance ended with his death.

In 732 B.C., Assyria marched on Damascus, capturing the city and killing King Rezin of Syria. A wave of deportations followed, and countless Israelites were removed from the land. Yet even with Assyrian control tightening, Hoshea tried to rebel by allying with Egypt, hoping to break free from foreign domination after Tiglath-Pileser III's death.

But Assyria's new king, Shalmaneser V, swiftly responded. He captured Hoshea and imprisoned him. The people of Israel fled behind the walls of Samaria, which held out under siege for three long years.

Finally, in 721 B.C., Samaria fell.

The last stronghold of the Northern Kingdom collapsed under the weight of foreign oppression and divine judgment. Its citizens were carried into exile, its buildings razed, and its land repopulated by Assyrian settlers. The kingdom of Israel was no more.

In the aftermath, the southern kingdom of Judah attempted to consolidate power and provided refuge for those who remained. But the message was clear: no political alliance, no foreign god, and no earthly strategy could replace faithfulness to the Covenant.

The fall of Israel marked the end of a nation that once bore the name of God, but chose instead to follow the ways of foreigners.

King Shalmaneser V of Assyria died in 722 B.C., just before the final fall of Samaria. His successor, Sargon II, completed the conquest of Israel and intensified the terror campaign that followed. The Assyrians didn't just conquer—they humiliated.

The high officials of Israel suffered gruesome, public executions: their noses, ears, and fingers were cut off to break their dignity and instill fear. Some had their eyes gouged out, while others were beheaded or burned alive. It was a message to all who would dare defy the Assyrian Empire: submission or annihilation.

Skilled workers, artisans, and nobles were rounded up and deported to distant regions like the Medes and other outposts across the Assyrian domain. Sargon II returned in 720 B.C., suppressing revolts and deporting another 27,290 Israelites—a final blow to the fractured northern kingdom. Their land was resettled with Assyrian citizens, completing the demographic and cultural shift.

The spiritual erosion deepened. Many of the Israelites who remained in the land began to worship the gods of Assyria, abandoning Yahweh. Intermarriage between Israelites and the newly resettled non-Hebrew populations further diluted covenant identity. Though some resisted, many submitted to integration. Others fled south into Egypt, or migrated deeper along the Nile River and into West Africa, giving rise to the enduring legacy of the Ten Lost Tribes.

King Hoshea, a puppet ruler, was the last king of northern Israel. After his imprisonment, Israel's identity as a sovereign, covenant people were shattered.

By 684 B.C., Sennacherib, another ruthless Assyrian king, faced a Babylonian uprising. In retaliation, he flooded the city of Babylon, turning it into a swampland and erasing its resistance with environmental devastation. The Assyrian war machine spared no one—neither rebellious Israel nor Babylon, Egypt, or Ethiopia.

The judgment was not only historical—it was prophetic.

"And the Lord rejected all the descendants of Israel, afflicted them, and delivered them into the hands of plunderers, until He had cast them from His sight."

(2 Kings 17:20)

And the message extended beyond Israel to Africa's great kingdoms.

The prophet Isaiah warned that even Egypt and Ethiopia—once centers of strength and refuge—would fall under Assyrian domination:

"Just as My servant Isaiah has walked naked and barefoot three years for a sign and a wonder against Egypt and Ethiopia, so shall the king of Assyria lead away the Egyptians as prisoners and the Ethiopians as captives, young and old, naked and barefoot, with their buttocks uncovered, to the shame of Egypt. Then they shall be afraid and ashamed of Ethiopia, their expectation, and Egypt, their glory."

(Isaiah 20:3–5)

This was a sobering warning to all nations that placed their trust in an empire, idolatry, or political alliances over obedience to the Creator. Yahweh was not only the God of Israel but the Judge of nations, and His call for covenant loyalty extended beyond borders and bloodlines.

After the death of King Ahaz, his son Hezekiah ascended the throne of Judah. Unlike his father, Hezekiah was a righteous king who immediately initiated a sweeping spiritual and national reform. He worked to restore the cultural identity and the covenant integrity of Judah, which had been eroded under the weight of Assyrian tribute and idolatry.

In the first year of his reign, Hezekiah repaired the house of the Lord, opened the doors of the synagogue for worship, and sent messengers across the land—including to the remnants of northern Israel—inviting them to join Judah in celebrating the Passover. He removed the wooden images and destroyed the bronze serpent that Moses had made, which the people had begun to worship as an idol.

Hezekiah understood what was at stake. The Assyrian empire loomed like a great shadow, casting a dark cloud over Afrocentric and Israelite lands alike, draining wealth through oppressive tribute and smothering faith under imported idols. But as Assyria's grip tightened, hope stirred from the south and the east.

During Shabaka's reign, the 25th Dynasty of Ethiopia conquered Egypt, burning the former ruler Bocchoris alive and expelling the lingering Aryan occupiers. With Egypt and Kush unified under Ethiopian rule, the powerful Kushite empire began to reclaim its influence, even annexing Philistia, near Judah's western border.

Meanwhile, in Mesopotamia, Merodach-Baladan, a prince of the Bit-Yakin tribe, returned to Babylon, assassinated the sitting ruler, and reclaimed the throne, momentarily establishing Babylonian independence from Assyria. To Hezekiah, this looked like a divine opportunity.

With Ethiopia rising in the south and Babylon resisting in the east, Hezekiah refused to continue paying tribute to Assyria and began preparing Judah for war. He revitalized the economy, restructured tax burdens, and took strategic military precautions. Knowing Sennacherib, the Assyrian king, would soon respond, Hezekiah constructed a tunnel through solid rock—now known as the Siloam Tunnel—to redirect water from the Gihon Spring into the city and cut off external access.

He also secured a treaty with the Ethiopian monarch, relying on the strength of the 25th Dynasty. At the time, Shabako ruled as king, and his relative Tirhakah was the military commander.

In 701 B.C., the anticipated clash came. From the hills of Eltekeh near the Mediterranean coast, the Kushite and Egyptian coalition launched a campaign to confront Sennacherib. The two massive armies—Assyrians and Kushites—collided with full force. Armed with bows, chariots, and elite cavalry, the Ethiopians fought fiercely alongside Egyptian forces.

Both sides suffered heavy losses at the city wall of Eltekeh, but logistical challenges quickly emerged. Hezekiah's decision to reroute Judah's water supply proved problematic for the Kushite army. Deprived of water for their troops and horses, they were forced to retreat.

Rather than chase the Ethiopians, Sennacherib turned his wrath on Judah's surrounding cities. He destroyed towns, dug ditches to sabotage irrigation, smashed tunnels, and burned settlements to trap civilians inside. His brutal focus shifted next to Babylon and Elam, who had participated in the broader rebellion. Merodach-Baladan, sensing the oncoming judgment, fled the city of Kish, preserving his life but leaving Babylon vulnerable.

The Assyrian empire struck back with vengeance, but cracks began showing. Though the Ethiopian offensive did not succeed militarily, it signaled the beginning of sustained resistance from Afro-Eastern powers. Hezekiah's defiance had inspired a spiritual and political stand—a declaration that Judah would no longer bow to the false gods and unjust systems of the empire.

After securing victories in Eltekeh, Erech, Tyre, Sidon, and other rebellious city-states, Sennacherib unleashed the full wrath of the Assyrian Empire. He executed the rulers and nobles who resisted or withheld tribute, seizing vast treasures of gold, silver, precious stones, livestock, and anything else of value. Once the cities were stripped of their wealth, they were set ablaze—left as smoldering warnings to all who dared defy Assyrian supremacy.

Sennacherib's armies swept into Ekron and pushed toward Judah, defeating the Ethiopian reinforcements that had arrived in hopes of defending the region. What followed was a campaign of terror. The inhabitants were slaughtered, their bodies impaled on stakes and displayed around the city walls to intimidate neighboring towns. From the central highlands to the Sorek Valley, Timnah, Mizpah, and the Euphrates basin, no community that resisted escaped Assyrian brutality.

Those who submitted quickly were spared but forced into subservience. These surviving city-states—Ashdod, Ammon, Arvad, Edom, Gaza, and Pelusium—sent lavish gifts to the Assyrian king: gold, silver, ivory, leather, precious gemstones, jewelry, and even the daughters of nobles as a token of total submission. They bowed, kissed Sennacherib's feet, and accepted servitude under the empire's heel.

But behind the Assyrian sword stood something even more dangerous: a racial and spiritual ideology.

The Assyrians believed they were led into battle by their chief god, Indra the Asura—a deity whose mission was the subjugation and destruction of all who opposed him, especially the darker-skinned Indigenous races. The military conquest was not just political; it was a sacred war of racial domination.

Encouraged by his mystical soothsayers and priests, Sennacherib moved forward confidently, deploying his heavy infantry and artillery to level fortified cities. Like other Aryan conquerors, the Assyrians imposed their language, culture, and gods on every people they subdued. Their campaign was one of cultural erasure—obliterating the sacred traditions, spiritual memory, and racial identity of the Indigenous populations.

The Assyrians fought with precision and fury, on horseback and in chariots, wielding long, two-handed swords for close combat and firing arrows from afar. Their destruction was systematic, but it was also religious.

The spiritual foundation of their violence is echoed in the ancient Rig Veda, the Aryan religious text:

"He verily, the god, the glorious Indra, hath raised him for man... brought low the dark head of the wicked Dasas... Indra, the Vritra-slayer, Fort destroyer, scattered the Dasa hosts who dwelt in darkness. To him in might, the gods have ever yielded... He slaughtered the Dasyus and cast down their forts of iron."

(Griffith, 2008)

These verses reveal the ancient worldview behind Aryan imperialism: that dark-skinned people—the Dasas and Dasyus—were enemies of the gods, destined to be crushed, enslaved, or exterminated. It was not just about land—it was about spiritual supremacy cloaked in racial warfare.

Sennacherib's conquests were, in essence, a living manifestation of this belief system. His campaign wasn't merely military—it was a religious crusade aimed at extinguishing Afro-Asiatic cultures, faiths, and identities that stood in opposition to Aryan dominance.

In the fourteenth year of Hezekiah's reign, Sennacherib intensified his assault on Judah, sacking 46 cities and 20 villages, including the key fortress of Lachish. In desperation, Hezekiah sent envoys to offer a massive tribute: 300 talents of silver and 30 talents of gold, hoping to appease the Assyrian king and halt the destruction (2 Kings 18:14).

But tribute could not quench the bloodlust of the Assyrian Empire.

The Kushite Alliance and Judah's Spiritual Trial

The Kushites—faithful allies of Judah—fought alongside them, but the effort proved overwhelming. Battle after battle wore them down, and despite the expectation that the Ethiopian army under Shabako would hold firm, they faltered in the heat of combat. Their strength was no match for the relentless advance of Assyria.

Though the Kushites had previously defeated Assyrian invaders in Egypt and expelled many Aryan occupiers, their victories could not stop the tide sweeping through Judah. The lesson was profound: opposing white imperial dominance in the Kushite sphere required more than physical might—it required spiritual allegiance to Yahweh, the God of the Covenant.

Sennacherib, swollen with pride, celebrated his victory in racial and spiritual terms:

> "I have brought the black-headed people in submission at my feet."

Yet the prophet Isaiah had already foreseen this moment. He warned Judah not to place their trust in the Ethiopian coalition, no matter how strong they seemed. Military might would not save them from the judgment that had already been decreed:

> *"Woe to those who go down to Egypt for help, and rely on horses, who trust in chariots because they are many, and in horsemen because they are strong, but who do not look to the Holy One of Israel, nor seek the Lord!"*

(Isaiah 30:1)

The defeat of the Kushite army left Judah isolated, its capital Jerusalem surrounded and trembling. Overwhelmed by fear and guilt, Hezekiah stripped the gold from the doors of the Temple, emptied the royal treasury, and sent it all to Sennacherib in apology. But it was not enough. The Assyrian king had conquered nearly all of Judah—only Jerusalem remained.

Standing outside its walls, Sennacherib mocked the city, praising the power of his god, Indra the Vritra-slayer, and boasting of his victories over the dark-skinned nations. But Isaiah did not waver. He urged the people to turn their eyes from defeat to heaven and cry to Yahweh for deliverance.

And Yahweh responded.

> *"Then Isaiah the son of Amoz sent to Hezekiah, saying, 'Thus says the Lord God of Israel: Because you have prayed to Me against Sennacherib king of Assyria, I have heard you.'"*

(2 Kings 19:20)

That very night, the angel of the Lord swept through the Assyrian camp, and 185,000 soldiers fell dead. When the people awoke the next morning, the once-unstoppable army of Sennacherib lay silent, corpses scattered across the landscape.

> *"And it came to pass on a certain night that the angel of the Lord went out, and killed in the camp of the Assyrians one hundred and eighty-five thousand; and when the people arose early in the morning, there were the corpses—all dead."*

(2 Kings 19:35)

Yahweh had not abandoned His people—He was waiting for their return, not to an empire or foreign alliances but to the Covenant. Judah had stood at the edge of annihilation, and it was not the strength of Ethiopia or the gold of the palace that saved them. It was a prayer and the power of God, who still fights for justice.

Manasseh's Reign—Spiritual Betrayal and Imperial Submission

After the death of King Hezekiah, his son Manasseh ascended the throne as the fourteenth king of Judah. Though he was only twelve when he became king, Manasseh would reign for fifty-five years—the longest reign in Judah's history. But his reign became infamous not for its longevity but its wickedness.

Manasseh abandoned the covenant legacy of his father and returned Judah to the idolatrous practices of his grandfather Ahaz. He ruled with the spirit of rebellion, embracing the Pagan customs of the surrounding empires and doing evil in the sight of the Lord.

In open defiance of Yahweh, Manasseh:

Built altars to the sun, moon, and stars—the astral gods of Babylon and Nineveh—within the inner and outer courts of the temple itself.

Reconstructed altars to Baal and created Asherah poles, just as Ahab, the corrupt king of Israel, had done before him.

Rebuilt the high places and altars to the lower spiritual realms—powers of darkness that his father, Hezekiah, had previously torn down.

Desecrated the holy house of the Lord, where Yahweh had declared, "In Jerusalem I will put My name."

One of the most heinous acts of Manasseh's reign was his participation in child sacrifice. He burned his sons in the fire as an offering to the god Molech in the Valley of Ben Hinnom—an abomination that represented the total rejection of divine life and justice.

In addition to blood sacrifice, Manasseh practiced witchcraft, soothsaying, and necromancy, consulting with familiar spirits and sorcerers—all practices strictly forbidden by Yahweh and deeply embedded in Babylonian and Assyrian occult traditions.

It was during this dark chapter that the prophet Isaiah, one of Judah's greatest voices, was sawn in half—a martyrdom carried out under Manasseh's tyrannical rule, according to Jewish tradition.

Manasseh also submitted politically to the Assyrian empire, paying tribute to Sennacherib and later to Esarhaddon, Sennacherib's son, who ruled over Babylon. Rather than resisting the empire's influence, Manasseh aligned himself with it economically, religiously, and spiritually, welcoming the gods and their systems of Assyria into the heart of Judah.

Manasseh's reign was not merely an administrative failure. It was a spiritual betrayal—a generational reversal of covenant, righteousness, and divine identity. He turned Judah into a kingdom of blood, sorcery, and idolatry, leading the people even further away from the Creator.

Despite the rich legacy of his father, Hezekiah, King Manasseh plunged Judah into one of its darkest eras—not only through idolatry and child sacrifice but also by aligning militarily with Assyria against Ethiopia, Judah's most trusted ally. This betrayal was more than political—it was spiritual. Ethiopia had long been a faithful partner, and much of Judah's gold flowed from Kushite-controlled regions like Ophir. Yet under Assyrian pressure, Manasseh turned his back on this long-standing alliance and participated in campaigns against his African kin.

Meanwhile, Sennacherib, the arrogant king of Assyria, met his end at the hands of his sons Adrammelech and Sharezer while worshiping in the temple of Nisroch (2 Kings 19:37). The assassins fled to Ararat, and Sennacherib's son, Esarhaddon, assumed the throne. Esarhaddon unified Assyria and Babylon and began restoring Babylonian infrastructure, but rebellion struck in his first year.

In a bold move, Babylon allied with Ethiopia, under the leadership of Tirhakah, king of the 25th Dynasty of Kush. Esarhaddon launched a campaign against Tirhakah in 674 B.C., only to suffer a humiliating defeat at Sais in Egypt.

Esarhaddon then turned his wrath on Judah. He captured King Manasseh, bound him in bronze shackles, and dragged him with hooks to Babylon. There, in a foreign prison, Manasseh finally humbled himself before Yahweh. His repentance was genuine. When he was released, he returned to Jerusalem and removed all foreign idols and altars from the temple, attempting to restore what he had once destroyed (2 Chronicles 33:11-15).

But Esarhaddon wasn't finished with Kush.

In 671 B.C., he returned to Egypt, capturing Memphis and taking members of Tirhakah's royal family—including his wife and son—as prisoners. Esarhaddon installed Necho I, ruler of Sais, as a puppet king under Assyrian control. Egypt was forced to pay tribute, and for a time, Kushite dominance in Lower Egypt was broken.

Esarhaddon's arrogance was unmatched. He declared:

"I am powerful, I am all-powerful, I am a hero, I am colossal... I am without equal among all kings, the chosen one of Asshur, Nabu, and Marduk."

(Walvoord & Zuck, 1983)

He allowed loyal local chiefs to retain their positions in exchange for opposition to Kushite power. But the resistance wasn't over.

Though pushed south, Tirhakah regrouped. Two years later, with support from local Egyptian rulers, he recaptured Memphis. As Esarhaddon prepared to respond, he was ambushed and killed by Ethiopian forces—a divine reversal in the struggle between imperial arrogance and Afrocentric resilience.

Esarhaddon's son, Assurbanipal, succeeded him and swiftly ordered the assassination of Egyptian leaders who had sided with Tirhakah. Yet resistance continued.

In 664 B.C., Tantamani, Tirhakah's nephew and the final king of the 25th Dynasty, launched a campaign to reclaim Egypt. He advanced down the Nile and killed Necho I, striking at the heart of the Assyrian-installed regime. But his victory was short-lived. Assurbanipal sent a massive force that overwhelmed the Kushite army, recaptured Memphis, and advanced to Thebes, looting treasures and desecrating temples.

The Assyrians installed Psamtik I, the son of Necho I, as ruler over Lower Egypt and enforced tribute. However, Upper Egypt remained under Kushite influence for another eight years. As punishment for resistance, many Egyptian and Nubian children, nobles, and citizens were captured and executed.

By 656 B.C., Psamtik I reunited Lower and Upper Egypt, ending Assyrian rule. Though he faced resistance from chiefs loyal to Kush, he stabilized his reign through military and economic alliances with Greece, founding Greek colonies and building a naval fleet that dominated the Mediterranean and Red Sea for over half a century.

CHAPTER 6

Babylon Rising Empire: Exile, and Spiritual Deception

As the mighty empire of Assyria began to crumble, Babylon's economy and influence surged at an accelerating pace. Babylon became a magnet for displaced populations—new arrivals mingled with the darker-skinned Natives of Nineveh, creating a volatile social and cultural environment. Meanwhile, the Medes grew in strength in the north, intently watching the faltering Assyrian grip.

The prophet Nahum called Nineveh the "city of blood," a haunting title that captured the cruelty of the Assyrians, who had ruled through terror: impalement, beheadings, the burning of children, and relentless suppression of Indigenous populations. These atrocities seeded rebellion in the hearts of the oppressed, many of whom were ready to rise alongside Babylon and throw off the yoke of Assyrian domination.

In 652 B.C., Shamash-shum-ukin, the Assyrian-appointed governor of Babylon, rose in open revolt against his brother Assurbanipal. But Babylon was starved into submission. To maintain control, Assurbanipal placed two of his relatives as co-governors of the city. However, the Assyrian grip would not last.

Following Assurbanipal's death in 627 B.C., a former Assyrian general named Nabopolassar seized the moment. Expelling Assyria's appointed governors, he crowned himself king of Babylon in 626 B.C., uniting the people under a new banner of resistance. He then allied with Cyaxares, the powerful king of the Medes, to begin dismantling the Assyrian Empire from the inside out.

Amid this power struggle, King Josiah of Judah made a fateful decision. Believing that Babylon might prove more sympathetic to the covenant people, Josiah aligned Judah with Assyria in the fight against Egypt, and Assyria's former adversary turned into an uneasy ally. Egypt, under Necho II, was advancing to aid the Assyrians at Carchemish near the Euphrates.

Josiah attempted to block Egypt's passage at Mount Carmel, determined to hold the line. But this decision proved fatal. At Megiddo, Josiah intercepted the Egyptian army despite divine warning. Necho sent word:

"What have I to do with you, king of Judah? I have not come against you this day, but against the house with which I have war; for God commanded me to make haste. Refrain from meddling with God, who is with me, lest He destroy you."

(2 Chronicles 35:21)

But Josiah pressed forward.

"So, he came to fight in the Valley of Megiddo. And the archers shot King Josiah; and the king said to his servants, 'Take me away, for I am severely wounded.'"

(2 Chronicles 35:22-23)

Wounded in battle, Josiah was carried back to Jerusalem, where he died from his injuries. His death marked the loss of a righteous reformer and the beginning of Judah's downward spiral into Babylonian control.

The Medes and Babylonians completed their mission. They stormed Nineveh, demolished the city, and sent waves of survivors into exile. Assyria was finished.

In Judah, Josiah was succeeded by his son Jehoahaz, but his reign lasted only three months. Necho II arrested him in Riblah, and Judah became a vassal of Egypt. Necho installed Jehoiakim, Jehoahaz's brother, as king—a puppet monarch who would soon answer not to Egypt, but to Babylon.

In the eighteenth year of King Josiah's reign, a monumental discovery shook Judah's spiritual core: High Priest Hilkiah found the "Book of the Law" in the temple. Its words validated the ancestral faith and historical covenant of the Jewish people, revealing just how far they had strayed.

Josiah was deeply moved by the text and grieved the nation's disobedience. He launched sweeping reforms: tearing down the altars of Baal, destroying Pagan images, and purging idolatrous practices, including sacred prostitution. He cleansed Judah and even the fallen land of northern Israel, striving to restore a unified standard of worship centered on Yahweh alone.

Though Josiah began ruling at just eight years old, he reigned faithfully for 31 years and is considered one of Judah's last righteous kings.

But his death marked the beginning of national decline.

Under his successor, King Jehoiakim, righteousness was quickly replaced with injustice and idolatry. Ruling from 609 to 598 B.C., Jehoiakim did evil in the sight of the Lord. Judah, weakened and indebted, fell under Egyptian control and was forced to pay heavy tribute. In this time of political submission and spiritual collapse, God raised the prophet Jeremiah to speak a final warning.

"Thus says the Lord: 'Stand in the court of the Lord's house, and speak to all the cities of Judah... Do not diminish a word. Perhaps they will listen and turn... then I will relent from the calamity. But if not, I will make this house like Shiloh, and this city a curse to all nations."

(Jeremiah 26:2–6)

Jeremiah's words enraged the priests and false prophets, who ordered the people to seize him. But Jeremiah stood firm:

"Do with me what seems right, but know this—I was sent by the Lord."

A few elders of Judah defended him, remembering the legacy of past prophets who warned of destruction.

God then gave Jeremiah a powerful symbolic mission: He was to wear a wooden yoke in public—an image of submission to Babylon. He also sent yokes and bonds to six surrounding nations allied with Babylon. These nations—Ammon, Egypt,

Moab, Edom, and others—had once been called "siblings" of Israel. But over the generations, they had betrayed the Covenant of Brotherhood, turning hostile toward the descendants of Abraham.

The Ammonites and Moabites descended from Lot's children. The Edomites were born from Esau's mixed lineage. All had, at various times, aligned with Israel's enemies.

While Jeremiah walked through the temple wearing the wooden yoke, a rival prophet named Hananiah stepped forward. In a public spectacle, he broke Jeremiah's yoke, delivering an opposing prophecy:

"Thus says the Lord: 'Within two years, I will break the yoke of Nebuchadnezzar from all nations!'"

But the Lord responded again through Jeremiah:

"You have broken the wooden yoke, but I will replace it with a yoke of iron. I have placed all these nations under Nebuchadnezzar, and they shall serve him."

Then Jeremiah turned to Hananiah and declared:

"The Lord has not sent you. You have made this nation trust in a lie... Therefore, you will die this year, for you have taught rebellion against the Lord."

And just as prophesied, Hananiah died in the seventh month of that year.

By 605 B.C., the geopolitical order of the ancient world had shifted. At the decisive Battle of Carchemish, Babylon crushed the combined forces of Assyria and Egypt on the banks of the Euphrates River. With that victory, Nebuchadnezzar seized control of key Egyptian territories, including Ashkelon, tilting the balance of power in his favor.

Faced with Babylon's rising dominance, King Jehoiakim of Judah chose temporary survival over covenant allegiance. He became a vassal of Babylon, agreeing to pay tribute in exchange for Judah's safety. As a show of dominance, Nebuchadnezzar deported Judah's royal family members to Babylon, including the young noble Daniel and his three companions: Hananiah, Mishael, and Azariah.

Upon arrival, their Hebrew names were stripped away, replaced with Babylonian titles:

Daniel became Belteshazzar,
Hananiah became Shadrach,
Mishael became Meshach,
Azariah became Abed-Nego.

This renaming was an attempt to erase their Hebrew identity and assimilate them into Chaldean culture, reflecting Babylon's deeper strategy—not only to conquer land, but to reprogram minds and rewrite their identity.

Meanwhile, Ethiopia was absent from the Carchemish campaign. Under Necho I and Psammeticus I, Egypt had cut ties with Ethiopia, fearing retaliation from Assyria. Still, many Egyptians defected to Ethiopia, seeking shelter under its more just and familiar rule, fueled by deep resentment over Assyrian brutality.

Though the Battle of Carchemish signaled the beginning of Babylonian supremacy, it also allowed Egypt to retreat and live to fight another day. Remnants of Assyrian forces and Philistine groups allied under Egypt's command, but they lacked the strength to repel Babylon fully.

Three years into his vassalage, Jehoiakim rebelled against Babylon and realigned with Egypt—a fatal mistake. In response, Nebuchadnezzar unleashed his regional allies: Chaldeans, Syrians, and Ammonites, who began attacking Judean towns. Egypt offered no protection, and Jehoiakim died before the final Babylonian assault.

The prophet Ezekiel was among the second wave of deported captives, carried away with thousands of others as Babylon tightened its grip.

Judah Captured

With Babylon's allies surrounding the land, Nebuchadnezzar prepared for the final blow. Before the siege began, Jehoiakim's son, Jeconiah, and the royal family and Judah's officers surrendered. In return, Nebuchadnezzar spared the city from immediate destruction but stripped the temple of its treasures and carried off all the sacred gold articles.

He then deported the royal court, military commanders, skilled craftsmen, and artisans, leaving behind only the poorest citizens to inhabit the broken land. Jeconiah's reign lasted only three months before he was sent into Babylonian captivity, marking the near-total collapse of David's dynasty.

After the exile of King Jeconiah, Nebuchadnezzar appointed Jeconiah's uncle Mattaniah as king, renaming him Zedekiah—a symbolic act of dominance that marked Judah's total subjugation. Yet even in this judgment, God revealed a deeper purpose to the prophet Jeremiah.

The Lord showed Jeremiah a vision of two baskets of figs placed before the temple. One basket held very good figs; the other, so bad they couldn't be eaten. The Lord explained:

"Like these good figs, so will I acknowledge those carried away captive from Judah, whom I have sent out of this place for their good... I will bring them back to this land... I will give them a heart to know Me, that I am the Lord."

(Jeremiah 24:5–7)

But for the "bad figs"—those who remained in rebellion:

"I will deliver them to trouble among all the kingdoms of the earth... to be a reproach, a byword, a taunt, and a curse in every nation." (Jeremiah 24:9)

Zedekiah ruled under Babylonian authority for nine years, swearing allegiance to Nebuchadnezzar. But internal pressure from religious leaders, nobles, and false prophets pushed him to revolt. Under a new Pharaoh, Egypt promised to support Judah, a familiar but unreliable ally.

When Zedekiah sought a word from the Lord, Jeremiah warned him plainly:

"Pharaoh's army will return to Egypt... and the Chaldeans will come again, fight against this city, and burn it with fire."

(Jeremiah 37:7–8)

Nebuchadnezzar's army surrounded Jerusalem, erecting siege walls. The famine was so severe that no bread was left for the people. At one point, when Babylon temporarily withdrew due to Pharaoh's advance, Jeremiah tried to leave the city, but was accused of treason and thrown into a dungeon.

Eventually, Zedekiah moved Jeremiah to the prison court. The king continued to seek Jeremiah's counsel in secret. The prophet repeated the hard truth:

"Whoever remains in the city will die by sword, famine, or plague. But whoever surrenders to the Chaldeans will live."

"This city will surely fall into the hands of Babylon."

(Jeremiah 38:2–3)

Jeremiah was later lowered into a cistern filled with mud and left to die. But a faithful Ethiopian eunuch named Ebed-Melech heard of the injustice. Risking his life, he approached the king and secured Jeremiah's release, lifting him out of the pit with the help of thirty men.

Once free, Jeremiah gave Zedekiah a final word:

"If you surrender to Babylon, you and your house will live, and the city will not be burned. But if you refuse, this city will be delivered to the Chaldeans, and they will burn it with fire."

(Jeremiah 38:17-18)

Zedekiah wavered—trapped between pride, fear, and public pressure. Though he once promised freedom to all Hebrew slaves, he revoked the covenant, enslaving them again, further violating divine law and sealing Judah's fate.

When the Babylonians returned, Zedekiah attempted a desperate escape under cover of night through a secret passage in the king's garden. But his flight ended on the plains of Jericho, where he and his royal household were captured.

They brought Zedekiah to Nebuchadnezzar. There, he was forced to watch the execution of his sons—a final sight before the Babylonians put out his eyes, bound him in bronze chains, and carried him to Babylon.

After Zedekiah's capture, the Babylonians sealed their conquest with brutality. They executed Judah's remaining political, military, and religious leaders, erasing the last remnants of resistance. Then, they looted the temple and royal palaces, stripping them of bronze, gold, silver vessels, and sacred items.

Once Jerusalem's prestige was dismantled, they set fire to the Temple of Yahweh, the king's palace, and every significant house in the city. Nebuzaradan, the captain of Nebuchadnezzar's guard, led the final deportation, taking hostages to Babylon, yet leaving behind the poor of the land to serve as vinedressers and farmers.

The prophet Nahum had once spoken of Ethiopia and Egypt—nations whose strength once seemed boundless:

"Ethiopia and Egypt were her strength, and it was boundless; Put and Lubim were your helpers. Yet she was carried away, she went into captivity... Her young children dashed to pieces; her great men bound in chains."

(Nahum 3:9)

Unlike Assyria, Babylon chose to establish its administrative center in Mizpah, not Jerusalem. They appointed Gedaliah governor. Meanwhile, Jeremiah, who had been imprisoned for preaching the truth, was found in chains and nearly carried away. But Nebuchadnezzar had heard of him.

He ordered Nebuzaradan to show Jeremiah kindness. The prophet was freed and told he could go anywhere he pleased—including Babylon, where he would be treated with honor. Because of his unwavering prophecies against Judah, Babylon saw Jeremiah not as an enemy but as a truth-teller.

As the dust of destruction settled, many Jews fled to Ammon, Moab, Edom, Ethiopia, and Egypt, seeking refuge from Babylon's wrath. Others returned to Judah upon hearing of Gedaliah's appointment. But their hope was short-lived.

With ten men, a resistance group led by Ishmael assassinated Gedaliah and the Babylonian-appointed officials. They also massacred Jewish civilians loyal to the new regime. Ishmael fled to Ammon, and many Jews fled once again to Egypt, fearing Babylonian retaliation.

Despite its brutality, Babylon—as the first true Aryan empire—allowed certain dark-skinned peoples limited participation in military, economic, religious, and political life. They could work as soldiers, farmers, artisans, and merchants; some could purchase their freedom. But Nebuchadnezzar still enslaved thousands, including Hebrews, to build his luxury palaces, grand monuments, and the Hanging Gardens.

In Scripture, Babylon becomes more than an empire—it becomes a spiritual archetype. In the Book of Revelation, it is "the great prostitute"—symbolizing the seductive power of wealth, prestige, and idolatry that draws nations away from the true God.

"Babylon, the great... the mother of prostitutes and the abominations of the earth."

(Revelation 17:5)

Babylon was the first kingdom called a beast in the Book of Daniel, representing imperial power that dominates through military conquest, economic manipulation, and spiritual deception. Babylon promised opportunity, even inclusion, but once it secured control, it betrayed its darker-skinned allies and oppressed them like the rest.

Its name, Babylon—meaning "Gate of the gods"—marks it as a spiritual stronghold. Many believe it to be the original city where fallen angels communicated with humankind, teaching forbidden knowledge and revealing the secrets of the unseen world.

As both the Koran and the Book of Revelation affirm:

"It is the devils who are unbelievers who taught mankind witchcraft and that which was revealed to the angels Harut and Marut in Babylon."

(Koran, Surah Al-Baqarah 2:102)

"So, the great dragon was cast out—that serpent of old, called the Devil and Satan, who deceives the whole world; he was cast to the earth, and his angels were cast out with him."

(Revelation 12:9)

Thus, Babylon was more than a city—it was a portal of deception, a spiritual empire rising repeatedly through history. It seduced with gold, enslaved with law, and exalted itself as divine—but it stood as the opposite of everything the Covenant nations were called to be.

Life in Exile: Faith and Culture in Babylon

After the destruction of Jerusalem and the exile of Judah's elite, the Hebrew people began to settle along the Chebar River, a broad waterway southeast of Babylon. There, they began to rebuild their lives in small colonies and municipalities. Despite their displacement, these exiles found ways to cultivate community, economy, and spiritual identity in foreign soil.

One of the most prominent exiles was King Jeconiah, who, after years of captivity, was eventually released by Evil-Merodach, the new Babylonian king. Jeconiah was shown royal favor and allowed to establish a residence in Nehardea, where he built a synagogue and became a close confidant of the king. Under his leadership, Jewish life in Babylon began to flourish, and Nehardea became a prosperous center of Hebrew culture and commerce.

Though many captives were allowed to move about freely and engage in trade, Babylon never let them forget who ruled. The Babylonians reinforced their spiritual supremacy through the exaltation of their gods, chief among them was Marduk, the divine patron of Babylon.

To display Marduk's power, the Babylonians constructed a massive golden statue, weighing over 44,000 pounds, depicting the deity seated on a throne. Marduk stood at the center of Babylonian religion, worshipped as the king of the gods, the god of order, and the guarantor of the empire.

One of the most important religious events was the Akitu Festival, held each spring to mark the Babylonian New Year. During the Akitu:

The Nebo (Nabu) statue—the god of wisdom, writing, and Marduk's divine son—was transported from Borsippa to Babylon's Esagila Temple.

There, in an elaborate ceremony, the statues of Babylon's major deities were assembled to represent divine communion and alignment of celestial forces.

Nebo was believed to lead the gods in reaffirming Marduk's supreme authority for the coming year, protecting Babylon from evil and chaos.

The high priests brought the Babylonian king before the statues of the gods. After undergoing purification rituals and surrendering his royal insignia, the king reaffirmed his divine right to rule, symbolically placing Babylon's fate in Marduk's hands.

The temple was purified, sacred offerings were made, and music, chants, incense, and theatrical rituals filled the air—each act a deliberate invocation of cosmic power. At the height of its spiritual arrogance, Babylon believed that through ritual, gold, and idol worship, it could manipulate the universe.

These ceremonies were not mere pageantry—they were theological statements of control, aimed at seducing conquered peoples into spiritual submission. And yet, amidst all this, the Hebrew exiles preserved their faith. Though surrounded by golden idols and forbidden mysteries, they remembered the God who spoke without image, whose throne required no gold, and whose presence was not confined to temples made by human hands.

Babylon's Festivals

One of the most spiritually revealing ceremonies in Babylon was the Bacchus festival, celebrated in honor of the birth of the son of the Queen of Heaven. Bacchus (also called Tammuz in Babylonian myth) was the god of wine, fertility, and sensual love, and his celebration was drenched in intoxicating ritual, sexual orgies, and symbolic acts of death and rebirth.

In Babylonian mythology, Ishtar—the so-called Queen of Heaven—was believed to have birthed Tammuz through a miraculous conception. His annual death and resurrection represented the seasonal cycles of nature. This mythos was central to the Bacchus festival—also known as the Drunken Festival—which included:

- Sacred sexual rites, where temple prostitution was considered a divine act to please the gods.
- Young women were expected to dedicate their virginity to the mother goddess through ritual intercourse.
- Wine, dance, and ritual intoxication symbolized the "purification" of sin.
- Slaves were temporarily emancipated and allowed to live freely during the five-day celebration.

The festival began around December 21, marking the winter solstice—a time symbolizing death and rebirth. During peacetime, celebrants wore purple robes, and in wartime, they dressed in leopard skins.

A key celebration feature was the evergreen tree, decorated with gold, silver, and ribbons, symbolizing eternal life and divine consciousness. A mistletoe branch was grafted onto the tree, representing celestial reconciliation. Gifts were exchanged, and sacred cakes or buns—called "boun"—were baked and offered to ancestral spirits.

"The children gather wood, the fathers kindle the fire, and the women knead dough, to make cakes for the queen of heaven... that they may provoke Me to anger."

(Jeremiah 7:18)

These rites were not isolated to Babylon. The Romans later incorporated similar practices in their Saturnalia (December) and Bacchanalia (March) festivals. In early Rome, the calendar had only ten months, with March as the New Year, until the Julian calendar introduced January and February in 46 B.C.

In 186 B.C., the Roman Senate outlawed the Bacchanalia, calling them wild, immoral, and destabilizing. Yet many continued to celebrate underground; over time, the rituals were reinstated under state supervision. These ancient festivals left a lasting imprint, reverberating even into modern holidays.

Today, Christmas carries many remnants of the Bacchus festival:

The evergreen tree, the gift exchange, and the winter solstice timing, and the central role of women in celebration and preparation—echoing the female-centric fertility rites of Ishtar.

In Daniel chapter 5, it was likely during this very Bacchus-style feast that Belshazzar, king of Babylon, hosted a grand celebration using sacred vessels stolen from the Temple in Jerusalem:

"Belshazzar the king made a great feast for a thousand of his lords... They drank wine and praised the gods of gold, silver, bronze, iron, wood, and stone."

(Daniel 5:14)

At the height of revelry and arrogance, divine judgment fell. A mysterious hand appeared, writing a prophetic message of doom on the palace wall. That night, Babylon fell to the Persian

Empire, led by Cyrus, who entered the city under the cover of darkness and redirected the Euphrates to breach its walls.

With all its splendor, gods, festivals, and mysticism, Babylon had been weighed and found guilty.

The city of Babylon stood as one of the most outstanding architectural achievements of the ancient world. It was fortified with eight bronze entrance gates, flanked by walls soaring 320 feet high and 80 feet thick, with a vast waterway completely encircling the city. The most prominent entrance was the Ishtar Gate—a monumental structure glazed in brilliant blue enamel bricks, intricately decorated with images of the lion, dragon, and bull—symbols of power and divine favor.

Leading to this gate was Processional Street, a grand ceremonial avenue running along the eastern side of the Southern Palace. The street connected to the Nabo Temple at its southern end, dedicated to Nebo (Nabu), the god of wisdom and writing. The main roadway between the walls was Aibur-shabu, meticulously paved with breccia limestone from distant mountains.

The sidewalks were inlaid with small, polished red stones, and the center of the road shimmered with larger limestone blocks. The route was built for imperial spectacle, designed to celebrate the gods and glorify Babylon's might.

Above the gates rose a seven-story watchtower, guarding the city's entrances and the riverbanks. Towering over the city skyline were the ziggurats—pyramid-shaped temples nearly 300 feet tall, serving as spiritual stairways to the heavens. The Southern Palace, including the Esagila Temple, functioned as a royal residence and the spiritual center of Nebuchadnezzar's empire.

The city's most legendary attraction was the Hanging Gardens, believed to have been cultivated on the terraced steps of the Southern Palace. Built to comfort a Median or Persian queen homesick for her mountainous homeland, the gardens featured cascading waterfalls, exotic trees, and flowering vines supported by massive marble and limestone pillars.

CHAPTER 7

Babylon's Splendor and the Prophecy of Empires

Babylon was a showcase of beauty, dominance, and luxury. Nebuchadnezzar brought the best artists, engineers, and thinkers from across his empire to build his vision, but African and Israelite slaves crafted these wonders. Though the king allowed some to purchase their freedom, the labor and skill of the enslaved were the backbone of Babylon's splendor.

In this environment of captivity and allure, many Hebrews found economic opportunity. Living between Babylon, Nippur, and Kish, they cultivated fertile land, became merchants, and even grew wealthy. Yet this prosperity came at a spiritual cost. Nebuchadnezzar's intention was clear—to seduce the Hebrews into becoming Babylonians and absorb them economically, culturally, and spiritually.

Many exiles, especially the younger generation, began to lose sight of their heritage. Their songs fell silent, and their traditions dimmed, but not all forgot.

From this pain and longing rose one of the most powerful laments in Hebrew Scripture—Psalm 137—a sacred poem of exile, memory, and resistance:

By the rivers of Babylon,
There we sat down, yea, we wept
When we remembered Zion.
We hung our harps upon the willows in the midst of it.
For those who carried us away captive asked us a song,
And those who plundered us requested mirth, saying,
"Sing us one of the songs of Zion!"
How shall we sing the Lord's song in a foreign land?
If I forget you, O Jerusalem,
Let my right hand forget its skill.
If I do not remember you,
Let my tongue cling to the roof of my mouth,
If I do not exalt Jerusalem above my chief joy."

Even in the heart of the empire, the remnant remembered. Even while walking the golden streets of Babylon, they mourned for Zion, covenant, and home.

Daniel's Dream and the Kingdoms

In the second year of his reign, King Nebuchadnezzar was shaken by a disturbing and mysterious dream, so profound it left his spirit troubled and restless. Though surrounded by priests, astrologers, and magicians who claimed divine insight, the king saw through their pretense. He refused to tell them what he had dreamed and demanded both the dream and its interpretation.

> "I have had a dream," he declared, "and my spirit is anxious to understand it." One of the Chaldeans stepped forward and replied in Aramaic—the court language of Babylon: "O king, live forever! Tell your servants the dream, and we will give the interpretation." However, Nebuchadnezzar, determined to expose their false claims, made an impossible demand: "My decision is firm. If you cannot tell me the dream and its interpretation, you shall be cut into pieces, and your houses shall be made ash heaps. But if you succeed, I will give you gifts, rewards, and great honour. Now, tell me the dream and its meaning."

Panic filled the royal court. The astrologers replied that no man on earth could do such a thing—only the gods, they said, could reveal it, and they do not dwell with flesh.

Enraged by their failure, Nebuchadnezzar ordered the execution of all the wise men in Babylon. The decree reached Daniel, one of the Hebrew exiles, and among the young men trained in Babylonian knowledge.

Daniel requested time to speak with the king. Then, with urgency and faith, he returned to his quarters and informed his companions: Hananiah, Mishael, and Azariah (Shadrach, Meshach, and Abed-Nego). Together they prayed for God's mercy and asked that the secret of the king's dream be revealed so that they might not perish with the rest of the wise men.

That night, God answered. The Lord revealed the dream and its interpretation to Daniel in a night vision. Immediately, Daniel praised the God of Heaven with a prayer of deep reverence:

"Blessed be the name of God forever and ever, for wisdom and might are His. He changes the times and the seasons; He removes kings and raises up kings. He gives wisdom to the wise and knowledge to those who have understanding. He reveals deep and secret things; He knows what is in the darkness, And light dwells with Him. I thank You and praise You,

O God of my fathers, You have given me wisdom and might, And have now made known to me what we asked of you, For You have made known to us the king's demand."

(Daniel 2:20-23)

At that moment, the God of Israel—not the gods of Babylon—was revealed as the trustworthy source of power, insight, and authority. This event would soon elevate Daniel from an outsider in exile to a prophetic voice inside the empire's highest courts.

After Daniel's prayer was answered, he immediately went to Arioch, the captain of the king's guard, and urged him to spare the lives of the wise men of Babylon. Daniel assured him that he could interpret the king's dream—not through any extraordinary wisdom, but by divine revelation.

Brought before Nebuchadnezzar, Daniel made it clear from the beginning: no man, no magician, astrologer, or soothsayer could reveal the king's secret. But...

"There is a God in heaven who reveals secrets," Daniel declared, "and He has told you what will come to pass."

Daniel humbled himself before the king, not as one with superior wisdom, but as a vessel:

"This secret has not been revealed to me because I have more wisdom than anyone alive, but so that the king may know the thoughts of his heart."

Then Daniel described the dream that Nebuchadnezzar had not even spoken aloud:

"You, O king, were watching, and behold—a great image!

This immense statue, dazzling in splendor, stood before you. Its appearance was awesome."

Daniel described the image piece by piece:

The head of the statue was made of fine gold.

The chest and arms were of silver.

The belly and thighs were bronze.

The legs were iron.

The feet were part iron and part clay—a fragile and unstable foundation.

Then Daniel spoke of something supernatural—a shift from metal to stone:

"You watched as a stone was cut out—not by human hands—and it struck the image on its feet of iron and clay, shattering them to pieces."

"Then the entire statue—iron, clay, bronze, silver, and gold—was crushed together and became like chaff on a summer threshing floor. The wind carried them away, leaving no trace. But the stone that struck the image became a great mountain and filled the whole earth."

"This," Daniel said, "is the dream." (Daniel 2:29-36)

In this vision, man's kingdoms—no matter how dazzling—are temporary. The stone, not cut by human hands, symbolizes a divine kingdom that was founded not by empires or elites but by God Himself. The dream is a prophecy of history unfolding and of the empire eventually falling before the mountain of God.

Daniel's interpretation of the king's dream revealed not just a mystery—it unveiled a prophetic blueprint for the rise and fall of world empires. He told Nebuchadnezzar that the head of gold represented Babylon, the first and most glorious of four Gentile kingdoms. The Lord had granted him dominion, power, and glory—but his reign was just the beginning of a larger prophetic cycle.

The Kingdoms After Babylon

Following Babylon, a second kingdom, inferior in splendor but powerful in its own right, would rise—the Medo-Persian Empire, symbolized by the chest and arms of silver. Then would come a third kingdom, represented by the belly and thighs of bronze, known for its rapid expansion and philosophical influence: the Greek Empire, emerging from the sea people—Indo-European Aryan tribes from the Balkans who had permanently rooted themselves in these ancient lands.

But the fourth kingdom—the legs and feet of iron—captured Daniel's attention with its terrifying strength and lasting legacy. This kingdom, which devoured and crushed all others, was none other than Rome. The legs of iron symbolized Rome's unmatched military power and enduring legal system. But its feet and toes, a mix of iron and clay, foretold its eventual fragmentation—strong, yet fragile, due to its internal divisions and moral corruption.

Daniel also saw this kingdom as a beast with four heads and ten horns. Unlike the other beasts, it was ferocious and unnatural, tearing through nations with iron teeth and trampling what remained underfoot. Among the ten horns, a little horn emerged, with eyes like a man and a mouth that boasted arrogantly. This horn rose quickly, surpassing the others and uprooting three rival horns in its ascent.

This "little horn" foreshadowed a spiritual-political power—a union of church and state that would speak "great things" against the Creator and oppress the Covenant People of God. Historically, the papacy in Rome played this role. Over centuries, it emerged from a complex legacy of justifying slavery, with the Pope eventually claiming both religious authority and significant political power throughout Western Europe, the Middle East, and Africa.

As Rome fragmented, the empire divided into ten regions—symbolized by the ten toes. These included the nations that emerged from its collapse, such as the Netherlands, Portugal,

France, Spain, Germany, Italy, and Britain. Each retained elements of Rome's iron nature—legalism, militarism, conquest—but none had the unity or strength of the original empire.

A new power—the United States of America—would later rise out of Britain, born from Rome's legacy and the British imperial order. Like Rome, the United States would come to symbolize military might, political dominance, and economic supremacy. It bore the eagle as its emblem, a symbol of imperial rule, just as Babylon and Rome had before.

The United States, the final expression of the iron-and-clay empire, inherited Rome's infrastructure, Greece's philosophy, Persia's governance, and Babylon's pride. But like all before it, it is fragile at the core—divided by race, caste, class, and corruption.

Daniel's vision showed that the stone "cut out without human hands" would strike not the head or chest of the statue, but the feet, the foundation of this entire Gentile system. And when the stone hit, the whole image collapsed, turning to dust and blown away by the wind, while the stone became a mountain that filled the whole earth.

This was the message to Nebuchadnezzar—and every future empire: No kingdom built on conquest, exploitation, or idolatry will last. Man does not make the kingdom that will endure, but by God Himself.

After Daniel interpreted the king's dream of the great image and the stone that shattered it, Nebuchadnezzar was overwhelmed. Humbled by the accuracy and insight of the interpretation, he fell on his face before Daniel—a rare act for a Babylonian king toward a Hebrew exile. He made Daniel chief ruler over all the provinces of Babylon, elevating him above the king's wise men, astrologers, and administrators.

Yet the revelation was far from complete.

Later, Nebuchadnezzar had a second dream—this one even more troubling. He described it to Daniel as a magnificent tree towering high into the heavens, visible from every corner of the earth. Its leaves were lush, and its fruit abundant. Beasts found shade beneath it, and birds nested in its branches—a symbol of prosperity and global influence.

But then, the king saw a holy messenger—a Watcher—descend from heaven, proclaiming:

"Chop down the tree and destroy it. But leave the stump and roots in the earth, bound with bands of iron and bronze, surrounded by the tender grass. Let him be drenched with the dew of heaven and live with the beasts of the field, until seven times pass over him."

The vision stunned Daniel. He was silent, astonished for a moment. Then he spoke—respectfully but truthfully:

"My lord, may the dream concern those who hate you. But it is you, O king. You are the tree."

Daniel explained that Nebuchadnezzar's greatness had grown to the heavens, and his dominion to the ends of the earth. But pride had infected the king's heart. Because of this, God would drive him away from people. He would live like an animal in the wild, eating grass like an ox and being soaked with the dew of heaven. This state would last seven years—until the king acknowledged that God rules over the kingdoms of men and gives them to whomever He chooses.

Daniel pleaded with the king:

"Break off your sins by practicing righteousness. Show mercy to the poor. Perhaps then your prosperity may be prolonged."

(Daniel 4:27)

But Nebuchadnezzar did not heed the warning. A year later, walking along the rooftop of the Southern Palace—with a view of the Esagila Temple, the Hanging Gardens, and the vast beauty of the empire—he looked over Babylon and declared:

"Is not this great Babylon that I have built by my mighty power for the glory of my majesty?"

Before the words had even left his mouth, a voice from heaven thundered:

"O King Nebuchadnezzar, your kingdom has been taken from you. You shall dwell with the beasts of the field. You will eat grass like oxen, and seven times shall pass over you, until you recognize that the Creator rules in the kingdom of men."

Immediately, Nebuchadnezzar lost his mind. Driven from the palace, he lived like a beast, his hair growing like eagle's feathers and his nails like bird claws. He wandered the wilderness in madness, a living parable of the fall of prideful kings and empires.

Nebuchadnezzar's Humbling and the Rise of Persia

The king remained in this state for seven years until his reasoning returned. Then he lifted his eyes to heaven and praised the God of Heaven:

"His dominion is an everlasting dominion,
And His kingdom endures from generation to generation... Now I,
Nebuchadnezzar, praise and extol the King of heaven, All of whose
works are truth, and His ways are justice. And for those who walk
in pride, He is able to be humble."

(Daniel 4:34-37)

Nebuchadnezzar's honor and kingdom were restored. His court and officials welcomed him back—but now, with a transformed heart. He had learned what all rulers must eventually face: that pride precedes downfall, and only humility before the Creator leads to lasting authority.

It took a second dream—and seven years of divine judgment—for Nebuchadnezzar to finally acknowledge that Marduk, Babylon's chief deity, was inferior to the Creator God. His reign lasted 43 years and was marked by grandeur, military conquests, and a humbling transformation.

After his death, the throne passed to his son Amel-Marduk (also known as Abilmathadachos), but his rule was short-lived. Eventually, the crown came to Nabonidus, who became Babylon's final monarch. Nabonidus married Nitocris, the daughter of Nebuchadnezzar, securing legitimacy through royal blood. Their son, Belshazzar, was elevated to Crown Prince and ruled in his father's absence.

According to the historian Herodotus, Nitocris may have descended from Egyptian royalty, possibly due to the Babylonian invasion of the Twenty-Sixth Dynasty in 569 B.C. Her mother was referred to as a widow, and Nitocris a bastard child, which suggests she may have been born to an Egyptian concubine taken as tribute after a military defeat. In that era, it was common for conquering kings to claim the wives and daughters of their enemies as symbols of domination, turning women into sexual concubines and humiliation.

While Nebuchadnezzar had exalted Marduk, Nabonidus introduced Sin, the moon god, as Babylon's official deity. This act ignited conflict with the Marduk priesthood, Babylon's religious elite. In a bold and controversial move, Nabonidus abandoned the capital, relocating his court to Tema, an oasis city in northern Arabia. There, he constructed temples in his ancestral region of Haran—the place Abraham's father, Terah, had once paused instead of continuing to Canaan.

"Your fathers...including Terah...dwelt on the other side of the river...and they served other gods."

(Joshua 24:2–3)

This decision was not only politically unwise but also spiritually symbolic. By choosing Haran—a place historically associated with stalled destiny and idolatry—Nabonidus stood in contrast to the majority of Babylon's faith journey. His absence from Akitu, the New Year festival where all gods were believed to commune, angered the priesthood and further alienated the people.

Nabonidus remained in exile for ten years, leaving Belshazzar to govern Babylon. But the empire was vulnerable to spiritual decay, political division, and misplaced confidence in past victories.

Meanwhile, once Babylon's ally, Persia, had united with the Medes. Cyrus the Great, a rising force, persuaded Darius (also known as Gobryas), the governor of Elam, to defect. Persia conquered the Medes, then turned its attention to Babylon. When Cyrus launched an assault on Opis, a city along the Tigris River, the region of Akkad, once loyal to Nabonidus, revolted. The rebellion was brutally crushed, and Sippar fell soon after.

Nabonidus fled. But Belshazzar remained in Babylon—oblivious, proud, and willfully blind to the collapse surrounding him.

As the Persian forces marched toward the capital, Belshazzar hosted a lavish banquet for his nobles, wives, and concubines. In a final act of arrogance, he ordered the golden vessels stolen from the temple in Jerusalem to be brought forth—holy items taken by Nebuchadnezzar during the sacking of God's sanctuary.

They drank wine from these sacred cups, mocking the God of Israel, and praising their own idols of gold, silver, bronze, iron, wood, and stone. It culminated centuries of idolatry, conquest, and spiritual rebellion.

Babylon—the empire of empires—had turned its back on the God who reveals dreams, humbles kings, and lifts nations. Its fate was sealed.

As the Babylonian Empire teetered on the edge of collapse, a supernatural message appeared to mark its end.

During Belshazzar's lavish feast—filled with arrogance and intoxication—a mysterious hand appeared, writing on the wall of the royal palace. The letters glowed as if etched by fire, and the king's knees knocked in terror. His countenance changed, and the atmosphere shifted. The music stopped. The laughter died. Panic spread.

Belshazzar summoned all the wise men of Babylon to interpret the strange writing, but none could decipher it. The queen mother entered, recalling that Nebuchadnezzar had once promoted a Judean prophet named Daniel, who could interpret dreams and reveal secrets.

Daniel was summoned. If he could interpret the writing, Belshazzar offered him riches, royal garments, and high rank—a promotion to a third ruler in the kingdom. But Daniel, unimpressed, replied:

"Let your gifts be for yourself, and give your rewards to another. Nevertheless, I will read the writing to the king and explain its meaning."

Daniel reminded Belshazzar of his grandfather Nebuchadnezzar's downfall—the pride that brought him low, the insanity that humbled him, and the restoration that followed his repentance. He rebuked Belshazzar for failing to learn from that history, choosing instead to mock the Creator by drinking from the sacred vessels taken from the temple in Jerusalem.

Then Daniel read the words etched into the plaster:

MENE – God has numbered the days of your kingdom and brought it to an end.

TEKEL – You have been weighed in the balances and found lacking.

PERES – Your kingdom is divided and given to the Medes and Persians. (Daniel 5:26-28)

That very night, the prophecy came to pass.

While Babylon partied, the Persian army rerouted the Euphrates River, digging canals and tunnels to lower the water level. With the river shallow, Persian soldiers entered beneath Babylon's massive walls. The gates—left unguarded—were opened from within. The city fell without a fight, and Belshazzar was killed. Nabonidus returned to chaos and was captured by Darius the Mede, his former governor.

This moment fulfilled Daniel's vision of the ram with two horns—the Medes and Persians—rising in strength:

"I saw a ram pushing westward, northward, and southward, so that no beast could withstand him... and he became great."

(Daniel 8:3–4)

The Medo-Persians, like the Babylonians, Assyrians, and Scythians, were Indo-European peoples—tribes that had migrated from the highlands of Europe into the rich lands of Mesopotamia and beyond. But, unlike the kings before him, Cyrus the Great came with a new kind of rule.

After uniting the Medes and Persians, and defeating Lydia in 546 B.C., Cyrus conquered Babylon in 539 B.C.—not through massacre, but with strategy and diplomacy. Unlike the Assyrians and Babylonians who relied on terror, slavery, and rape, Cyrus abolished forced labor, outlawed sexual violence during festivals, and granted religious and cultural freedom to the peoples he conquered.

To the Jews in Babylon, Cyrus was not a conqueror, but a liberator.

He became the first Aryan ruler to institute a human rights charter, a document that protected the rights of all ethnic and religious groups within his empire. He allowed displaced people to return to their homelands, and under his decree, the Israelites were permitted to return to Jerusalem and rebuild their temple.

Centuries earlier, the prophet Isaiah had named Cyrus by name, long before his birth, declaring that God had anointed him for this mission:

"Thus says the Lord to His anointed, to Cyrus, whose right hand I have held... I will open the double doors so that the gates will not be shut... You may know that I, the Lord, who call you by name, am the God of Israel."

(Isaiah 45:1–5)

This was not just the fall of a city; it was the end of an era. The golden head of the statue—Babylon—had fallen. And now, the chest of silver—Medo-Persia—would rise.

But even this kingdom, righteous in its beginnings, would be tested. Every empire, no matter how enlightened, would eventually face the same question that Babylon ignored:

Whose kingdom will endure forever—man's or God's?

After Cyrus the Great's death, his son Cambyses II assumed the Persian throne. Where Cyrus had ruled with tolerance and respect for his conquered cultures, Cambyses quickly diverged into a path of arrogance, cruelty, and conquest.

His primary target was Egypt—a land rich in culture, wealth, and African legacy. By 525 B.C., Cambyses launched an invasion. Egypt, already weakened by internal strife, had employed Greek and Carian mercenaries—a defense strategy first introduced by Psammeticus I to resist Assyrian aggression. Though the Egyptians fought valiantly, they suffered heavy losses and retreated to Memphis. Cambyses pursued them into their sacred temples, where the Egyptians surrendered without resistance, and Egypt was annexed into the expanding Persian Empire.

But Cambyses' ambitions didn't stop in Egypt.

He turned his attention to Ethiopia, sending envoys under the pretense of friendship, bearing gifts for the king. In truth, they were spies, sent to assess the land's strength and wealth. But the Ethiopian king saw through the deception and exposed Persia's imperial intent:

"Your king is not a just man. If he were, he would not covet land that is not his, nor bring slavery upon a people who have done him no harm." (Herodotus)

In a striking gesture of defiance, the Ethiopian king handed the Persian spies a massive bow and declared:

"Tell your king: When the Persians can string this bow with ease, then let him give thanks to the gods that it has not entered the hearts of Ethiopians to covet foreign lands."

The message was clear—Ethiopia would not be subdued easily.

When the spies returned and delivered the Ethiopian king's insult, along with stories of scarce but sacred riches, including ivory, gold, myrrh, and fine copper, Cambyses was enraged. He launched a military expedition southward, determined to punish the land he could not conquer with diplomacy. His army set fire to the Oracle of Zeus-Amun, symbolically attacking the divine authority that guarded Ethiopia and North Africa.

He also sent expeditions toward Ammon and Carthage, but his plans were thwarted when the Phoenicians—new allies of Persia—refused to attack Carthage due to deep ancestral ties and oaths of kinship.

As the Persian forces advanced into the Desert of Ammon, they were overtaken by a violent sandstorm that buried the soldiers at mid-meal, erasing 50,000 men in an instant. Those who marched toward Ethiopia fared no better. As food ran out, the troops resorted to eating wild herbs, then each other. Reports of cannibalism reached Cambyses, and he retreated in disgrace, never having set foot in Ethiopian territory.

While little survives about the full extent of Cambyses's reign, ancient sources—including Herodotus and other historians—paint a picture of a ruler haunted by paranoia and moral decay. After his failed campaign, Cambyses's rule spiraled further. He allegedly married one of his sisters and ordered the assassination of his brother due to rising popularity. Later, he killed his younger sister as well.

One of the unspoken motivations behind Persian aggression toward Egypt may have been Cambyses's obsession with Egyptian women. He took an Egyptian concubine, and many Persian soldiers followed suit, enslaving and exploiting Egyptian women as part of their spoils of war. The conquest brought not only military domination but also racialized sexual violence, deeply wounding the African cultural and familial structures that had withstood centuries of external threat.

The Rise of Greek Civilization

The Greeks, who called themselves Hellenes, descended from a coalition of Aryans known historically as the Sea Peoples. These were Indo-European nomads who migrated from the Caspian Sea region into Crete and the Aegean coast. Originally fierce, horse-riding warriors, they had mastered stalking animals and war and brought these tools into the Mediterranean world.

One of the earliest Aryan tribes to settle in the region was the Dorians, who established dominance across Thessaly, the Peloponnesus, and parts of Asia Minor. They invaded Mycenae and Crete, burning settlements, razing temples, and displacing or enslaving the original non-Aryan inhabitants. With their expansion, more of their kin followed, and the Aryan presence in the Aegean grew.

The Minoans of Crete, one of the most advanced and peaceful civilizations in early history, became targets of this conquest. The Minoans were a blend of Israelite and Kushite ancestry, having migrated from the continent of Africa and parts of Asia to the Aegean Islands. Their capital, Knossos, stood as a testament to Afro-Semitic excellence—lavish palaces adorned with murals, sophisticated architecture, and vibrant depictions of daily life. They were master seafarers, forging trade networks with Egypt, Spain, North Africa, and beyond.

The Minoans developed an aquatic engineering marvel centuries before, channeling fresh water through aqueducts and underground drainage systems. Their society was remarkably practicing equality: women held positions of power, and cities had no fortified walls, reflecting a culture built on peace, not war.

But that peace would be shattered.

Around 1500 B.C., a massive volcanic eruption near the island of Kalliste (modern-day Santorini) triggered a catastrophic tsunami, decimating Minoan cities. Waves as high as 300 feet crashed onto Crete, killing nearly 40,000 people and crippling the civilization. As the Minoans struggled to recover, Aryan invaders from the north struck. They seized control of the island and established a new monarchical order built on domination.

The Aryans appropriated Minoan shipbuilding technology, transforming Crete into a launching pad for maritime conquest. With captured vessels, they became the feared Sea Peoples, waging war across the Mediterranean. The surviving Minoans fled to the Karfi Mountains, watching their cities and civilization fall under foreign rule.

Aryan conquest wasn't just physical—it was spiritual. They believed their gods had ordained their expansion, justifying war, enslavement, and the erasure of Afro-Semitic culture. According to their myths, these deities traveled with them, guiding and blessing their campaigns. Their goal was not coexistence, but replacement.

Thus began the Aryanization of the Aegean, marking the beginning of the Mediterranean's transformation into a battlefield of race, religion, and empire.

By the twelfth century B.C., a new wave of Aryan invaders—composed of Aeolians, Ionians, Sabines, and other Indo-European tribes—swept into southern Asia Minor and the Aegean Islands. These were not aimless wanderers. They came with a cultural agenda: to occupy, assimilate, and rule. Unlike their predecessors, who razed cities to the ground, these Aryan settlers found something different—a thriving civilization they saw as more valuable than ruins.

They encountered the remnants of the Minoan world, a civilization built by a Kushite-Israelite ancestry, still brimming with architectural brilliance, complex trade networks, and advanced infrastructure. The Minoans had built multistoried administrative centers, laid out paved streets with underground sewage systems, and designed ornate palaces filled with hieroglyphic-inspired murals. Their cities reflected a deep knowledge of engineering, art, and order.

Rather than destroy it, the new Aryan settlers absorbed and inherited the Minoan legacy. What would later be romanticized as "Greek innovation" was Minoan ingenuity repackaged. From classical columns to urban planning, murals to maritime trade logistics, the Greeks borrowed heavily from the Minoan-Kushite blueprint, often without acknowledgment.

As the centuries passed, these borrowed innovations were institutionalized into the Greco-Roman aesthetic, sanitized of their African and Semitic roots, and claimed as white European heritage.

CHAPTER 8

The Rise of Alexander and the Age of Empire

By 338 B.C., the legacy of conquest and appropriation reached its next chapter with the rise of Alexander the Great. At just 18 years old, he led the Macedonian cavalry under his father, King Philip II, at the Battle of Chaeronea. This pivotal victory unified the fragmented Greek city-states and the Aegean under Macedonian dominance.

This moment signaled not only a shift in political power but also the beginning of a global campaign of racial and cultural supremacy. Alexander's coming conquests would stretch across Africa and Asia, reinforcing the Aryan colonial blueprint established centuries earlier: conquer the land, rewrite history, absorb the culture, and erase its origins.

Building and Losing Alexander's Empire

Two years after commanding the cavalry at Chaeronea, Alexander became king when his father, Philip II, was assassinated by one of his bodyguards. Almost immediately, Thebes rebelled against Macedonian control. Alexander responded with brutal efficiency—he demolished the city and sold its inhabitants into slavery as a warning to any other dissenters.

Determined to fulfill his father's vision, Alexander launched a full-scale invasion of Persia, aiming to unify the so-called "brilliant West" with the ancient riches of the East and cultural depth.

In 334 B.C., he led 35,000 troops across the Hellespont into Asia Minor and won a surprise victory against Persian forces at the Granicus River. After the Greek reconstruction of the conquered cities, colonization increased. Greek military domination merged with the artistic and technological brilliance of the East, but always on Greek terms.

After taking Syria, Alexander sent envoys to Jerusalem to demand surrender. The Jewish high priest, Jaddua, and the elders refused. As Alexander approached the city to enforce submission, something unexpected happened. When he reached the gates, he saw Jaddua dressed in sacred white robes laced with purple and gold.

In a stunning moment, Alexander dismounted and bowed. He recognized Jaddua from a dream—God had shown him this encounter and foretold of Greece's rise to power. The same vision had been given to Jaddua, whom the Lord had instructed to meet Alexander in peace. In reverence, the Macedonian army withdrew without a single fight.

By 333 B.C., Alexander clashed again with Persian King Darius III at Issus. After routing the Persian army, he turned his attention to the strategic Phoenician city of Tyre. He laid siege to the island fortress for seven grueling months, eventually building a massive land bridge using cedarwood from Lebanon. When Tyre finally fell, Alexander executed 2,000 prisoners and sold the rest into slavery.

In 332 B.C., he marched across the Libyan desert, claiming Kushite territories along the Nile. But when he reached the border of Ethiopia, he stopped. There, Queen Candace, seated upon her war elephant and ready for battle, met him with a show of strength. Alexander turned away without a fight, unwilling to risk a campaign against such a formidable Black monarch spearheaded by a woman.

He shifted his campaign to the coast, battling Persian troops near Gaza. The Greeks broke through the city's defenses with siege towers and battering rams, and once inside, street fighting ensued until the Persians were overwhelmed.

In Egypt, Alexander was welcomed as a liberator from Persian rule. The Egyptians crowned him, Pharaoh. He founded the city of Alexandria on the Mediterranean coast—a symbol of Greco-Macedonian dominance, built on land first cultivated by African civilizations.

After crossing the Syrian Desert, Alexander the Great confronted King Darius III of Persia near Gaugamela and Arbela, just east of the Tigris River. In one of history's most decisive battles, Alexander's forces defeated the Persians. Darius was later killed by his men as he attempted to flee.

With Persia's leadership in disarray, Alexander swiftly seized control of Babylon and the ancient city of Susa, looting their royal treasuries. When his forces entered Persepolis, they raided the palace and burned it down—symbolically erasing the legacy of the Persian Empire. For the next three years, Alexander continued his campaign of conquest and colonization before dying of a sudden illness in Babylon at just 32 years old.

After his death, his empire fractured. His four top generals—the Diadochi—divided the kingdom, giving rise to smaller empires rooted in domination, exploitation, and imperial legacy. The Book of Daniel symbolically foresaw this rise and fragmentation, reflecting a divine perspective on human empires built through violence and arrogance:

"The male goat grew very great; but when he became strong, the large horn was broken, and in its place four notable horns came up... and out of one of them came a little horn which grew exceedingly great..." (Daniel 8:8-9)

Rome eventually emerged from a humble agrarian society into a dominating world power. Like the Greeks and Macedonians before them, the Romans were descendants of Indo-European migrants who came down from the hills of Europe. These early Aryan settlers, with their militarized caste systems, forcibly expanded into lands already inhabited by Indigenous peoples, especially darker-skinned communities along the Mediterranean and North Africa.

Although the Romans claimed to bring "order" through republican ideals, their version of civilization was deeply rooted in conquest, exclusion, and systemic inequality. Poor citizens were barred from military service due to the cost of armor, while elite Romans extended their power through forced labor, territorial seizure, and cultural erasure.

As Rome consolidated power over the Italian peninsula, it absorbed nearby communities, installing Roman law while enforcing imperial domination. Soldiers became settlers, policing the lands they conquered, expanding the empire in the name of "civilization"—a word often used to justify the dehumanization of others.

The Roman conquest of Magna Graecia, Campania, the Etruscans, and the Samnites reveals more than a thirst for territory—it reflects a deep need to prove dominance and assert divine entitlement to land. Rome expanded aggressively, masking its imperial ambitions behind religious justification and a belief in racial superiority inherited from the Indo-European Aryan worldview.

From Alexander to Rome: The Struggle for Mediterranean Power

By the third century B.C., Rome encountered North African Carthage, a powerful Phoenician civilization with deep African roots and a thriving multicultural society. While trade between the two nations initially brought mutual prosperity, Rome's appetite for control soon outweighed diplomacy. Carthage, concerned with Rome's rising military influence, became a target.

The Carthaginians had long defended their African and Mediterranean trade networks, including the culturally rich and racially diverse island of Sicily. Sicily and Syracuse were renowned centers of wealth, trade, and mixed-race culture, values that Rome saw as a threat to its racial and political hegemony.

When King Hiero II of Syracuse allied with Rome, it signaled the beginning of the First Punic War. Rome's colonial objective was to dominate Sicily, Sardinia, and Corsica—strategic islands crucial for trade and military access to Africa. The war lasted 20 years, claiming over 100,000 Roman lives and more than 700 warships. It also marked Rome's first major colonial land grab outside the Italian Peninsula.

Carthage fought fiercely to protect its sovereignty and culture, but Rome's hunger for global supremacy undermined its power. The tide nearly turned when Hannibal Barca, the son of Hamilcar Barca—an African general from Carthage—rose up with a diverse coalition of warriors and 37 elephants, crossing the Alps to challenge Rome directly. His multiracial army defied expectations and shattered Roman myths of invincibility.

Hannibal's campaigns across Italy, especially at Lake Trasimene, Trebia, and the Battle of Cannae, demonstrated tactical brilliance and Afro-Semitic resilience. At Cannae alone, Hannibal's forces killed over 25,000 Roman soldiers in one of history's most devastating military defeats. His strategic encirclement of 80,000 Roman troops exposed the vulnerability of the empire when met with tactical unity among colonized people.

Cities like Cannae, Capua, Syracuse, and Taranto—previously under Greco-Roman rule—rose and joined Hannibal, rejecting Rome's racial and cultural domination. This resistance was not only military but symbolic, challenging the narrative that white Aryan conquest was inevitable or divinely ordained.

As Rome expanded across the Mediterranean, its hunger for power brought it into direct conflict with Carthage, a wealthy African metropolitan founded by Phoenicians. What began as a trade relationship turned into a violent campaign of conquest, as Rome sought to dominate the seas and control the lucrative ports of Sicily and North Africa.

The First Punic War exposed the Roman Empire's early taste for imperialism. Despite losing over 100,000 men and hundreds of ships, Rome seized Corsica and Sardinia from Carthage, laying the foundation for its overseas empire. Carthage, a multiracial and multicultural society, was one of the few African powers capable of checking Rome's expansion. But Rome wanted more.

For a moment, it looked as if Africa would defeat Europe.

But Rome's empire was not built on merit—it was built on persistence, privilege, and a belief in its divine right to rule. Even as Hannibal won battles, Carthage refused to send reinforcements, fearing Rome's retaliation and placing internal politics above African unity.

While Hannibal tried to liberate those oppressed under Roman rule, most of Italy stayed loyal to the empire. It was a painful lesson: systemic oppression had become normalized. Rome's grip on power was not just military—it was psychological.

Hannibal's brother, Hasdrubal, was intercepted and killed. Meanwhile, a young Roman general, Scipio Africanus, took the war to Carthage. Rome's invasion of African soil forced Hannibal to return home and defend his people. At the Battle of Zama in 202 B.C., Scipio defeated the African general using Hannibal's strategies against him.

Rome forced Carthage to surrender its navy, relinquish all foreign territories, and pay tribute. Though Hannibal was allowed a political role, it was clear: Africa had been silenced, and Europe had claimed victory—not just militarily, but ideologically.

Scipio Africanus returned to Rome as a hero of the people, but the elite resented him for supporting land rights for poor farmers, many of whom had lost everything while fighting Rome's wars. The wealth gap widened, and Rome's republic slowly became an empire.

Rome's rise was not divine—it was a conquest rooted in inequality, racial subjugation, and theft of African brilliance. Hannibal's story reminds us that white imperial power has always feared and fought against unified Black resistance.

"His power shall be mighty, but not by his power; he shall destroy fearfully... and through his cunning, he shall cause deceit to prosper..." —

Daniel 8:24-25.

Destruction and Resistance in Rome's Expansion into Africa

The Third Punic War was ignited not out of necessity, but out of greed and white supremacist domination, and after rebuilding from earlier devastation, Carthage, an African economic power, thrived under Hannibal's leadership. He rooted out corruption, restored agriculture, and promoted coastal trade, rebuilding Carthage into a regional powerhouse. Though Carthage complied with Rome's humiliating treaty—surrendering its military, paying all debts, and requesting Roman mediation for border conflicts—Rome ignored every gesture of peace.

Instead of honoring the agreement, Roman Senator Cato fanned the flames of racial resentment. Disturbed by how quickly Carthage had recovered, he repeatedly ended speeches with "Carthage must be destroyed," weaponizing propaganda to justify another war. Rome's genuine concern was not peace, but the success and independence of a Black-led nation that proved it could thrive without European control.

In 149 B.C., Rome declared war on Carthage, claiming it had broken its treaty by defending itself from constant Numidian aggression. Rome demanded hostages and weapons, which Carthage handed over. Then, Rome moved the goalpost, demanding that the city be abandoned and rebuilt inland, away from the sea, severing Carthage's economy. It was a deliberate tactic of erasure.

When Carthage refused to destroy itself, Rome laid siege for three years, starving the population. In 146 B.C., Rome broke through and unleashed a genocidal massacre—killing over 600,000, raping women, burning infants alive, and enslaving the survivors. Once a symbol of Black excellence and innovation, the city was completely obliterated. Libraries were burned, and Carthaginian culture, history, language, and identity were almost entirely erased.

This was more than war—it was racialized annihilation. The aim was to make an example of Carthage and to permanently suppress African resistance to white imperial dominance. Even after Carthage's destruction, Rome continued its violent expansion. It raided Corinth in Greece and moved against Numidia (modern Algeria), where Jugurtha resisted Roman conquest.

Jugurtha's military brilliance humiliated Rome, but Roman officials eventually outmaneuvered him through bribery and diplomatic cunning. The neighboring kingdom of Mauretania betrayed him, and its ruler handed Jugurtha over to Sulla, commander of the Roman legion. In a final act of humiliation, the Romans paraded him through the streets in chains, still wearing his royal garments, before throwing him into a prison cell where he slowly starved to death.

Rome restructured its military to maintain control, allowing poor men to join for the first time, desperate citizens who fought not for justice, but for a slice of imperial spoils. This shift allowed Rome to colonize more African and Mediterranean lands, spreading its ideology of racial and cultural supremacy.

By 31 B.C., the Roman Civil War culminated in the Battle of Actium, where Octavian defeated Mark Antony and Cleopatra. Rome declared war on Egypt not just because of politics but also because of fear—a Black queen ruling one of the richest nations was unacceptable to the white imperial worldview. Cleopatra's death by suicide marked not just the end of a dynasty but the loss of another independent African nation.

Rome annexed Egypt and exploited its grain, oils, and labor resources to feed its empire. When Rome pushed further south into Kushite territory, Queen Amanirenas met them with force. Her army destroyed Roman garrisons, crushed the statue of Caesar, and humiliated their military so thoroughly that Aelius Gallus, the Roman commander, took his own life. Rome was forced to accept a new border—proof that Black resistance could halt imperial power.

For unto us a child is born, unto us a son is given,
And the government will be upon His shoulders...

(Isaiah 9:6)

Yeshua Ha'Mashiach—known in the West as Jesus Christ—was born in Bethlehem, a small town in Palestine, just south of Jerusalem. From the moment of His birth, He was targeted for death. The dark-skinned child became a refugee, forced to flee His homeland due to government-sponsored genocide aimed at eliminating black male infants. His family sought refuge in Northeast Africa and resided in southern Egypt.

Africa became the earliest sanctuary for Christ. God chose Egypt, a historically Black land, to protect His Son. It became home to some of the earliest Christian communities. The Coptic Christians of Egypt—descendants of this legacy—represent one of the oldest Christian traditions in the world.

Jesus was called "Yeshua," meaning "salvation," and given the title Ha'Mashiach— "The Anointed One." In Islam, He is known as Isa ibn Maryam, a prophet and messenger of God. Meanwhile, in Hinduism, the Aryan concept of Brahma evolved from older African spiritual systems and the god of the Indigenous Black populations of India, whom the Aryans later enslaved under their caste system. Brahma—later deified—was once the god of the original African Shudras and Dasas.

Jesus was born into a land under foreign occupation, controlled by the expanding Roman Empire. Rome, like many colonizing forces before and after it, brought violence, exploitation, and white supremacy disguised as civilization. In 63 B.C., Roman General Pompey invaded Judea and forced both Syrians and Jews into submission. But resistance had deep roots. In 164 B.C., a Jewish priest named Mattathias sparked a revolution by refusing to worship the Greek god Zeus. His sons, the Maccabees, led a revolt and won temporary independence.

However, Rome crushed that freedom. In 40 B.C., Rome installed Herod, an Idumean loyal to Rome, as ruler of Judea. To maintain his grip on power, Herod executed members of his own family. When he heard rumors of a prophesied child-king, he issued a violent decree to kill all infant boys in Bethlehem—another act of genocide against a marginalized population.

The Bible says Rachel wept for her children "because they were no more" (Jeremiah 31:15). This is not just a poetic lament. It is a historical cry of a people repeatedly subjected to colonization, forced migration, and racialized violence.

Yeshua's ministry directly challenged the empire. He didn't come with armies or political alliances. Unlike prophets before Him—like Moses, who became a general in the Ethiopian army, or Nehemiah, who rode into Jerusalem with a Persian military escort—Yeshua entered Jerusalem humbly, on a donkey. He ministered to the oppressed, healed the sick, uplifted the poor, and exposed the hypocrisy of power.

CHAPTER 9

The Revolutionary Message of Yeshua and the Rise of Empire

In a world obsessed with dominance, Yeshua's message was revolutionary: justice, love, healing, and truth—not for the powerful, but for the brokenhearted, the marginalized, and the colonized.

During this era, the Roman Empire exercised harsh political and social control over Palestine, deeply impacting Jewish life. Nazareth was a small, overlooked village in comparison to Galilee, a region where Jesus grew up under the shadow of systemic oppression. From a young age, He witnessed the brutality of Roman occupation and the deep divisions created by the caste-like system that rewarded silence and submission, even among His people.

As a young man, Yeshua Ha'Mashiach—known in the West as Jesus—emerged as a defender of the poor and marginalized. He challenged Roman supremacy and the complicity of elite Hebrews who had benefited from systemic injustice. His movement was not just spiritual—it directly threatened the religious and economic order. It exposed the greed, racism, and caste structures that kept the majority oppressed while rewarding the privileged few.

Yeshua, a dark-skinned Palestinian Jew, was invited to speak at the Capernaum Synagogue in Nazareth, where He had spent His youth. The city, known for its cultural beauty and Roman officials, was called "Galilee of the Gentiles"—a land under colonial control. Fulfilling the prophecy of Isaiah, Yeshua stood before the people and read:

"The Spirit of the Lord is upon Me, because He has anointed Me to preach good news to the poor.

He has sent me to heal the brokenhearted, to proclaim freedom for the captives and recovery of sight for the blind, to set the oppressed free, to proclaim the year of the Lord's favor."

After reading, He declared, "Today, this Scripture is fulfilled in your hearing."

This was a radical message for a divided people. The Jews were a minority in their homeland, both physically and spiritually bound by colonialism. The Gentiles—especially Roman elites—controlled the region but absorbed parts of the local culture, all while imposing their Eurocentric worldview and violent caste order.

Once moved by Yeshua's gracious words, the crowd quickly turned skeptical. "Isn't this Joseph's son?" they asked, unable to see past His humble beginnings. They failed to grasp the revolutionary message behind His sermon—a message that threatened the very structure of caste, privilege, and systemic oppression that ruled their lives.

Sensing their doubt and resistance, Yeshua delivered a bold and piercing response, recounting how during a great famine, the prophet Elijah was not sent to help an Israelite widow, but a Gentile woman in Sidon. And how, during Elisha's time, no leper was healed—only Naaman, a foreign commander from Damascus. Naaman served under a Gentile ruler. Naaman was struck with leprosy, turning his skin white as snow.

These words struck deep. Yeshua was exposing how God's grace was never exclusive to the powerful, the privileged, or even those with a particular ethnic identity. He was indicting the social order—both Roman and Israelite—that had grown comfortable with injustice. He was condemning their obsession with privilege and their silent complicity in a system built on the backs of the oppressed.

The people were enraged. They turned into a mob, dragged Him to the edge of the city, and attempted to throw Him off a cliff. But Yeshua passed through them and walked away unharmed. Some believe God blinded the mob in that moment. Others say Yeshua looked them in the eyes and walked directly through their hatred, unbothered and unbroken.

Early Christianity and the Fight for Inclusion

Yeshua Ha'Mashiach, the dark-skinned Palestinian Jew, came not only to liberate His people, but to confront the world's obsession with supremacy. Even the Aryan Gentiles, Balkan settlers who used race and caste to dominate Indigenous lives, were included in the call to repentance. Yeshua's gospel was radical—it rejected violence and taught love for enemies, while exposing the cruelty of the empire, racism, and religious hypocrisy.

His teachings disrupted the system. In a society where dark skin was equated with inferiority, where Romans called enslaved people andrapodon— "animals with the feet of men"—Yeshua reminded the crowd that whiteness was not holiness. Leprosy was not purity, but a curse. When referencing Naaman in the synagogue, he directly rebuked those who idolized Roman culture and power.

Naaman had been a servant of Ben-Hadad, king of Syria. Though he bowed in the Temple of Rimmon, a pagan god, the Lord struck him with leprosy. Even after being healed, the descendants of Gehazi, Elisha's servant, were cursed with the disease "white as snow" for exploiting God's gift for personal gain (2 Kings 5:27).

Yeshua was not just preaching salvation—He was dismantling the idol of racial hierarchy, calling out caste injustice, and revealing that God's kingdom was open to the oppressed, the foreigner, and the rejected. It was a movement that called for both liberation and accountability.

The Universal Father, the Highest Power, revealed Himself through Yeshua Ha'Mashiach (Jesus the Messiah) to offer salvation to the Hebrews and all people, especially those marginalized and forgotten by society. His mission crossed ethnic, national, and class boundaries. He came to dismantle systems of injustice and supremacy, not uphold them.

Yeshua's gospel of love, equality, and liberation challenged the deeply entrenched social caste system of the Roman Empire. His peaceful resistance exposed the greed and violence that maintained the status quo. Many Jews hoped for a militant savior, but Yeshua preached nonviolence, justice, and spiritual revolution. This approach enraged religious and political leaders alike.

When given the choice, the people, pressured by fear and manipulated by Roman ideology, chose to release Barabbas, a well-known insurrectionist, instead of Yeshua. This choice was shaped by survival under occupation and fear of Roman retaliation.

Meanwhile, the Apostle Paul, a Roman citizen born in Jerusalem, became one of the most influential voices in early Christianity. He traveled across the Roman Empire, including Greece, Ephesus, and Asia Minor, building diverse, multicultural faith communities grounded in liberation and unity. His longest letter, the Epistle to the Romans, was written while staying in Corinth—a multiracial, economically booming city of 500,000 people.

In Corinth, people from different cultures—Greeks, Romans, Egyptians, and Indigenous Cretans—came together. Paul's movement welcomed those from the bottom of society, including formerly enslaved people and outcasts. His collaborators—Titius Justus, Aquila, Priscilla, and Lydia—financed his mission, showing how women and working-class believers played a crucial role in building the early church.

Paul traveled with Luke, the only Gentile writer of the Bible, who documented their journeys in Luke and Acts. Paul rebuked false prophets and denounced sorcery and Pagan traditions that exploited the people. His ministry in Ephesus and beyond centered on justice and spiritual empowerment.

Eventually, Paul was executed during Emperor Nero's reign in 68 A.D., a martyr for the message he preached—a message that directly opposed the imperial forces of Rome, symbolized in Daniel's vision of the "iron kingdom that crushes all others" (Daniel 2:40). This imagery reflected the ruthless might of empires that rose by conquest and sustained their power through fear, slavery, and systemic inequality.

The Roman Empire tried to unify East and West, but its power was built on the backs of enslaved people. While some Africans and Jews rose in influence, the system remained exploitative at its core. The Roman world was exposed to monotheism through Judaism and early Christianity, transforming their religious worldview—but not their oppressive social order.

The empire's slave economy was brutal. Enslaved people— mostly Africans, along with prisoners from Germany, Russia, and Spain—were stripped of humanity and sold on auction blocks. Roman elites used them in agriculture, mining, construction, and even the arts. In the mines, conditions were deadly; enslaved people were whipped, starved, and worked to death for the sake of economic gain.

Rome's prosperity was built on colonization, forced

labor, and racialized systems of violence, much like the systems of white supremacy and caste oppression that exist today. Yeshua's gospel message still speaks: liberation for the oppressed, healing for the broken, and truth in the face of any empire's wishes.

Under Roman rule, slavery became the backbone of the empire's economy, but it was also one of the cruelest systems in history. Many enslaved people—especially those captured from Africa—were stripped of their dignity, auctioned off like livestock, and forced into backbreaking labor in fields, mines, construction, or domestic service. Women were often relegated to sexual servitude or domestic labor, while rebellious enslaved men were sometimes castrated or crucified as a warning to others.

One of the most brutal examples of Rome's inhumanity was in 71 B.C., when 6,000 enslaved people were crucified along the Appian Way after joining Spartacus in a failed rebellion. Even as some Roman laws were eventually passed to offer limited protections, these were more about preserving order than affirming humanity.

By 212 A.D., Roman citizenship was extended to all free inhabitants of the empire, including many who were once enslaved. Some used this status to buy freedom for themselves and their families, slowly climbing the social ladder. As formerly enslaved people gained education and wealth, they began to pose a threat to the upper class, who had built their privilege on the backs of the oppressed.

The rise of Africans in Roman society is a powerful testament to resilience and resistance. Among them was Septimius Severus, the first Roman emperor of African descent, born outside the empire. Severus was born in Leptis Magna (modern-day Libya). He ruled the empire for 17 years and implemented military and political reforms that challenged the elitism of the Roman aristocracy. Severus disbanded the Praetorian Guard—Rome's elite bodyguards—and replaced them with field-commanded military units, shifting power away from aristocratic senators and toward commanders with direct loyalty from the provinces.

Under his rule, Africans gained more influence, and the centralized control of Rome gave way to a broader and more diverse military force. Severus's rise to power showed the potential of African leadership in a system that had long worked to suppress and exploit darker-skinned peoples. Yet even he had to navigate a legacy of oppression—his predecessor, Julianus Severus, was of mixed African heritage but had ruled harshly against Africans and Jews, showing how proximity to whiteness often came at the cost of turning against one's own.

Rome's obsession with domination and racial hierarchy mirrors later colonial systems. The state's reliance on African labor, the dehumanization of darker peoples, and the eventual backlash of resistance reveals a repeating pattern across empires.

Isaiah's words echo across time, reminding us of the spiritual cost of rejecting the covenant:

"The labor of Egypt and the merchandise of Cush and the Sabeans, men of stature, shall come over to you...they shall bow down to you...All of them shall be ashamed and disgraced; they shall go in confusion together."

(Isaiah 45:13-16)

This passage doesn't just predict a dramatic reversal of fortune—it also makes clear that shame is the unescapable result of unjust power. In the end, the empire that turned its back on the covenant couldn't outrun its moral accountability.

The Atlantic Slave Trade and the Fight for Freedom

In one of the earliest biblical narratives, Cain, Adam and Eve's firstborn, killed his younger brother, Abel. Cain was a farmer; Abel was a shepherd. God accepted Abel's offering, but not Cain's, because Cain approached without faith or preparation. This rejection sparked jealousy and violence. As punishment, God cursed Cain, stripping him of his ability to farm the land and marking him with a skin condition—what some ancient texts describe as a form of leprosy. Cain became a wanderer, exiled to the land of Nod.

Over generations, Cain's descendants lived in harsh northern climates—what would become the Caucasus Mountains and the Balkan region. In these rugged lands, survival meant learning to hunt, trap, and raid. This nomadic lifestyle fostered a militaristic mindset rooted in survival, conquest, and unyielding unity. As time passed, these exiled descendants, now adapted to colder, barren territories, migrated south and began to war against the Afrocentric civilizations from which they had once come from.

This historical and spiritual conflict between those who cultivated the land and those who lived by conquest shaped the earliest dynamics of white supremacy and caste-based domination. The children of Cain returned with vengeance to raid, enslave, and destroy a people who never saw them as enemies—God's first fruit of the human family, the dark-skinned descendants of Abel, who had remained in divine alignment with the Creator.

This narrative reflects the deeper historical pattern of colonizers, often shaped by scarcity and trauma, projecting that pain onto peaceful, prosperous nations. The early Hebrew people, with their covenant to God, were treated as prey. Their communities were infiltrated, their bodies commodified, and their women violated—all under systems designed to strip them of identity and worth.

The curse placed upon Cain was not just a personal punishment—it became a generational affliction, driving conquest, division, and dehumanization. As the Hebrew people remained rooted in God's law and love, their enemies, formed in bitterness, pride, and violence, spread across the Earth, carrying spiritual venom that still poisons our systems today.

To truly understand systemic racism, colonization, and global inequality, we must return to these ancient fault lines. They reveal how cycles of violence were born—not just from human sin, but from the refusal to honor justice, humility, and the divine order that valued life over domination.

After the collapse of the Roman Empire, international trade declined, and with it, the demand for slave labor. The once-mighty empire had relied heavily on the wealth of conquest, but each European territory struggled to survive as it fractured.

In 1415, Portuguese prince Henry the Navigator sent

emissaries to explore the wealth of Africa. They seized Ceuta, a Moorish port on the North African coast. The Romans had long depended on Africa for grain and olive oil—once trade, later tribute. In a post-Roman world, Europe looked again to Africa, not for partnership, but for exploitation.

Portugal became the first European nation to re-enter Africa after the Middle Ages. When they arrived on the West African coast, particularly in Ghana, known as the Gold Coast, they were welcomed by African rulers who were open to trade. Ghana had developed a rich civilization with agriculture, complex trade networks, and vast resources. The Portuguese came not just for commerce but with intentions shaped by greed and racial superiority.

Africans introduced Europeans to crops like coconuts, yams, corn, millet, sugarcane, and spices. But when Europe discovered sugar, it craved cheap labor to cultivate it, and slavery became the engine of the colonial economy. The Portuguese king instructed his ambassadors to persuade African leaders to supply enslaved people. What followed was a brutal wave of betrayal. African families—mothers, fathers, and children—were torn apart and sold like cattle. Many were marched to European forts along the coast to await shipment into bondage.

The Portuguese built forts and slave depots along the coast, turning coastal Africa into a marketplace for human trafficking. Colonies like Cape Verde and São Tomé became early hubs for sugar cultivation, worked by enslaved Africans under European control.

When African rulers couldn't meet the European demand for human labor, Arab and Moorish raiders stepped in. These raiders, often mixed in ancestry, adopted European racial hierarchies, believing their lighter skin made them superior to darker Africans. They too became agents of white imperialism, participating in night raids, kidnappings, and village burnings to capture human beings for sale.

Islamic beliefs were sidelined in favor of profit. The Arab-Portuguese alliance thrived on division. They weaponized tribal differences, stirring conflict to prevent unity and resistance. They sowed mistrust among kin, leaving Africans vulnerable to betrayal and capture.

This calculated destruction of African unity—by both Europeans and their Arab intermediaries—laid the foundation for centuries of white supremacy. Under the guise of trade, what unfolded was a system of economic violence and racialized enslavement that continues to haunt the modern world.

Once captured, African men, women, and children were bound—hand shackled in iron, feet tied, and necks yoked together by bamboo. The Arabs, acting as middlemen for European buyers, marched these captives through dense forests for miles before delivering them to European traders waiting along the coast. The human cargo was then sold into slavery, initiating a centuries-long system of brutal exploitation.

"Then the Lord will scatter you among all peoples... there you shall serve other gods, which neither you nor your fathers have known— wood and stone. And among those nations you shall find no rest... but there the Lord will give you a trembling heart, failing eyes, and anguish of soul."

(Deuteronomy 28:64-66)

By 1492, the transatlantic system of oppression expanded further west. That year, Christopher Columbus—sailing for the Spanish Crown—set out searching for a trade route to Asia but arrived in the Caribbean instead. Welcomed by the Indigenous Taino people, Columbus and his crew were offered land, food, and help constructing settlements. The island, later called Hispaniola, would become the epicenter of genocide.

Columbus named his first settlement La Navidad, in what is now Haiti. Mistakenly believing he had reached India, he referred to the Native people as "Indians." The Taino showed immense hospitality, but that goodwill was soon betrayed. Columbus returned on a second voyage in 1493 to find his settlement destroyed. The Indigenous people had resisted enslavement and exploitation.

In response, Columbus unleashed a brutal crackdown. His men, armed with guns, crossbows, and steel swords, burned villages, accused the Taíno of plotting against them, and executed Queen Anacaona—the leader of the resistance—by hanging her before her people. She was only 29. After this, the Spanish began calling Indigenous peoples "savages" to excuse their violence.

Colonial expansion continued. Spain established La Isabela (present-day Dominican Republic) and Yaguana (near modern-day Léogâne, Haiti). Columbus's wealth reported triggered a rush of European settlers, who were granted land and protection by Spain's monarchs, Ferdinand and Isabella. Many Natives fled to the forests, while colonists took over their lands in search of gold.

Spain and Portugal formalized their colonial ambitions

with the Treaty of Tordesillas, dividing the globe into two spheres of conquest—Africa and the Americas. Once again, Indigenous hospitality was met with greed and genocide. Spain imposed a colonial system based on capitalism for whites, enforced by forced labor, religious indoctrination, and racial hierarchy.

Catholic missionaries converted entire communities by force. Indigenous cultures were erased. People were worked to death in mines, fields, and construction sites. The Spanish even trained dogs to hunt down and maul those who resisted. Any chief who refused to pay tribute—gold, copper, or crops— was punished. Some had their hands, ears, or noses cut off as public warnings.

Within 50 years, Spanish colonizers had exterminated nearly four million Taino people. Countless others in Cuba, Jamaica, and across the Caribbean fell to the sword, were torn apart by dogs, or died from European diseases like swine flu. With no natural immunity, entire villages disappeared. Farmlands were seized. Survivors were forced to worship the Spanish king and the Catholic Church—or die.

> *"So, they worshipped the dragon who gave authority to the beast, and they worshipped the beast, saying, 'Who is like the beast? Who is able to make war with him?'... and he caused as many as would not worship the image of the beast to be killed."*
>
> (Revelation 13:4, 15)

The Americas, like Africa, became a battlefield where white supremacy was enforced through religion, violence, and economic greed. The so-called "civilizing mission" of Europe was, in truth, a genocidal conquest built on systemic racism and the deliberate erasure of Indigenous and African cultures.

With the so-called "discovery" of the Americas, the transatlantic demand for enslaved labor exploded. The Indigenous populations of the Caribbean and the Americas were decimated by genocide, starvation, forced labor, and disease brought by European colonizers. As Native communities collapsed, European powers turned to Africa, fueling the largest forced migration in human history—the Atlantic slave trade.

Millions of Africans, mainly from West Africa, were captured, sold, and transported in chains across the ocean to work on plantations for the white ruling class. These captives labored endlessly on farms producing tobacco, cotton, coffee, cocoa, corn, peanuts, and other staple crops that enriched Europe. Enslaved Africans were also forced to maintain the homes of their captors—cleaning, cooking, laundering, and caring for their enslavers' families, often under cruel and dehumanizing conditions. Their cultural worlds were dismantled to make way for white supremacy.

African and Indigenous communities were torn apart. Once-thriving societies became fragmented into smaller villages, living in fear of raids, kidnappings, and colonization. The land's richness—its fertile soil, lush forests, and clean water—became both a blessing and a curse, exploited by European empires seeking wealth at any cost.

Saint-Domingue, the western portion of Hispaniola (modern-day Haiti), became the richest colony in the West Indies through brutal sugarcane plantations, cattle ranching, and mining, all powered by African slave labor. As wealth flowed from the Americas and Africa, European powers waged war over territory. The Roman Catholic Church often acted as mediator, negotiating control over African and American lands under the guise of divine right and Christian conversion.

By the 1600s, the French, British, and Dutch had followed Spain and Portugal into the Caribbean. In 1625, France seized parts of Tortuga and the Hispaniola mainland. Britain captured Jamaica in 1655, turning Port Royal into a haven for pirates who helped disrupt Spain's dominance. These European powers formed shifting alliances, using violence to protect economic interests and enforce racial hierarchies.

In 1657, the French and British allied to push Spain out of western Hispaniola. Under the 1795 Treaty of Basel, Spain formally ceded the territory to France, renamed it Saint-Domingue. The island became a center of European conflict, with Indigenous peoples fleeing into the mountains to escape colonial violence.

In the mid-1700s, MacKandal, an African-born, one-armed freedom fighter, led a powerful rebellion. Organizing maroon communities, he created poisons from native herbs to kill plantation owners and their families. MacKandal's underground resistance killed over 6,000 whites before he was betrayed, captured, and executed publicly. Yet his rebellion inspired future generations.

By the late 1700s, revolutionary flames spread. 1792 French official Leger-Felicite Sonthonax arrived to suppress slave uprisings, but the movement could not be contained. The American Revolution of 1776 inspired many white colonists to seek independence from France, while enslaved Africans and maroons fought for complete emancipation.

In 1802, Napoleon Bonaparte sent 20,000 troops, led by his brother-in-law General Charles Leclerc, to crush the Haitian resistance and restore slavery. Leclerc collaborated with white colonists and some free mulatto elites, including Alexandre Pétion, to reassert white supremacy. However, the movement for freedom in Haiti would only grow stronger and irreversible.

Haiti's Revolution and Its Leaders

Alexandre Pétion, born to a French colonizer and an African mother, was trained in France before rising to prominence in Haiti. During the Haitian Revolution, many mixed-race individuals, freed because of their kinship to white enslavers, initially supported Napoleon. The French exploited these divisions, weaponizing skin color and social status to prevent unity among the oppressed.

Despite this, Pétion eventually broke from the colonial structure and became one of the earliest Haitian officers to rebel against France. He joined leaders like Toussaint Louverture, Jean-Jacques Dessalines, and Henri Christophe in the revolutionary struggle. Pétion would later become the first president of independent Haiti.

In 1803, under the pretense of diplomacy, Napoleon invited Toussaint Louverture to a meeting, only to have him arrested by Jean-Baptiste Brunet. Louverture was deported to France, imprisoned in the Jura Mountains, and died by starvation. His capture further galvanized the Haitian generals and soldiers, who vowed never to return to slavery.

Napoleon responded to the rebellion with horrific violence,

including burning people alive, boiling victims in molasses, and hanging soldiers upside down to drown. Haitian women were lured to a midnight ball only to be informed of their husbands' executions. These atrocities helped unify Black, mixed-race, and Indigenous communities in their fight for liberation.

Some white Polish soldiers defected and joined the Haitian cause, fighting under Dessalines. By November 1803, the French were decisively defeated, and many colonists fled. The Haitian victory marked a pivotal blow to Napoleon's global ambitions, contributing to France's sale of its North American territories in the Louisiana Purchase.

Those white settlers who refused to leave were executed, while others were exiled. Dessalines redistributed wealth from French colonists to Haitian soldiers as reparations for the war. After Dessalines' assassination in 1806—allegedly orchestrated by Pétion and Christophe—the island split. Pétion led the south, representing the mixed-race population, while Christophe led the Black north.

By 1809, the island was divided into governance. Pétion ruled the southern republic until he died in 1818. The Spanish later reclaimed control of eastern Hispaniola, while the western side reclaimed the Indigenous name "Haiti," meaning "Land of Mountains."

Despite their revolutionary success, Haiti was denied international recognition by the United States, France, Spain, and Great Britain. These nations, driven by racism and fear of a successful Black republic, imposed devastating sanctions and demanded reparations that crippled Haiti's economy for generations:

"When He opened the fourth seal, I heard the voice of the fourth living creature saying, 'Come and see.' So, I looked, and behold, a pale horse. And the name of the man who sat on it was Death, and Hades followed with him. And power was given to them over a fourth of the earth, to kill with the sword, with hunger, with death, and by the beasts of the earth."

(Revelation 6:8)

The rise of European wealth and global power was built on the exploitation of African and Indigenous lives. Yet their violence was cloaked in the language of God and civilization. The system they created was not divine but demonic—a white supremacist caste structure designed to dominate and dehumanize.

Charles Darwin's "survival of the fittest" theory in The Origin of Species became a scientific justification for this brutal hierarchy:

"When beneficial to the individual, that gives rise to all the more important modifications of structure, by which the innumerable beings on the face of this earth are enabled to struggle with each other, and the best adapted to survive."

This logic echoed the mindset of Satan in his rebellion against heaven—a worldview rooted in domination, not divinity. European colonizers believed their right to conquer came from their power to kill, manipulate, and exploit, reinforcing a deadly hierarchy of human worth.

But Africa and the Americas had thriving, complex civilizations long before European arrival. Their downfall was not due to inferiority but a coordinated effort to divide, displace, and destroy. The caste system that emerged from this horror was crafted to elevate whiteness while devaluing everyone else.

We must name this evil. The global caste system—like the Hindu caste hierarchy and white supremacy—was a mechanism of control and cruelty. It sowed division, sanctioned genocide, and fueled war under the pretense of progress. Most enslaved Africans arrived in the Americas through the brutal Middle Passage—packed in ships like cargo, beaten, diseased, and treated worse than animals.

This was not merely history. It was a global crime against humanity, and its legacy remains alive in systemic racism, generational poverty, and institutional injustice. The time has come to confront that legacy with truth and accountability.

CHAPTER 10

The Middle Passage and the Foundations of Systemic Oppression

The Middle Passage was one of the most brutal chapters in the history of systemic oppression. Enslaved Africans were packed into the dark, poorly ventilated lower decks of slave ships—treated like cargo, stripped of dignity, and denied basic sanitation. Many captives were chained together and forced to lie in their filth. Those who resisted or refused to eat were beaten, and in some cases, sailors used iron tools to pry open their jaws to force-feed them. Women often watched in horror as their children were thrown overboard as punishment or to instill fear.

During the journey to the Americas, some captives attempted to jump overboard in desperation, choosing death over slavery. Those caught were whipped, branded, or burned. Suicidal acts became so common that ship crews treated them as routine disobedience, responding with even more cruelty. Upon arrival, those who survived the 3,000-mile voyage were branded with hot irons, marked like property, and subjected to psychological conditioning designed to break their will and erase their identity.

Olaudah Equiano, an African boy who survived the Middle Passage and later became an abolitionist, wrote: "The white people looked and acted, as I thought, in so savage a manner; for I had never seen among any people such instances of brutal cruelty."

He questioned the morality of the enslavers who called themselves Christians:

"O ye nominal Christians! Might not an African ask you, 'Learned you this from your God, who says unto you, do unto all men as you would men should do unto you?' Is it not enough that we are torn from our country and friends, to toil for your luxury and lust of gain?"

African women were especially vulnerable to sexual violence aboard these ships. Rape was rampant, and enslaved girls and women were repeatedly assaulted by white crewmen. Their cries and the moans of the dying turned the ships into floating houses of horror. Any children born of these assaults were often enslaved as well, seen as threats to white dominance, especially if they could pass for white. Mixed-race children were often targeted with even more brutal treatment to erase any notion of equality or kinship.

John Newton, a former slave trader who later became a Christian abolitionist, described the horrors he witnessed:

"When the women and girls are taken on board a ship, naked, trembling, terrified—perhaps almost exhausted with cold, fatigue, and hunger—they are often exposed to the wanton rudeness of white savages... perhaps some hard-hearted pleader may suggest, that such treatment would indeed be cruel, in Europe; but the African Women are Negroes, Savages, who have no idea of the nicer sensations which obtain among civilized people."

Newton's conversion was one of the rare moments of moral reckoning among those who had profited from slavery. But for millions of Africans, the damage was already done—etched into generations through trauma, dehumanization, and systemic racism that continues to echo through the present day.

This was not simply inhumane treatment; it was a global crime. The Middle Passage was not an anomaly—it was a calculated system built on racial terror, justified by religion, and protected by power.

Foundations of Racial Oppression

By 1518, the transatlantic slave trade intensified as a Spanish ship brought the first Africans to the Americas. With the Indigenous population decimated by genocide, disease, and forced labor, Europeans turned to Africa to fuel their growing colonial economies. The rise in sugar demand created a need for vast plantations and forced labor. Before sugar, honey was Europe's primary sweetener, but sugar quickly became the engine of economic transformation—and exploitation.

Plantations across the Americas grew crops like sugarcane, tobacco, cotton, and wheat, requiring intense manual labor. Europeans traded guns, alcohol, and manufactured goods for African captives, creating a violent cycle of human trafficking. The enslaved were stripped of their humanity, compared to beasts, while white supremacy was rationalized as divine will. A rigid racial caste system emerged, positioning whiteness as superior and embedding generational dehumanization into law, religion, and culture.

Similar to the Hindu caste system, where the darkest-skinned people were labeled "Untouchables" and excluded from society, Blackness became a global marker of stigma. This manufactured racial hierarchy blamed the oppressed while glorifying the oppressor. It was a spiritual and psychological assault, designed to obscure truth and justify brutality.

As Yeshua warned in John 14:30, "the ruler of this world is coming, and he has nothing in Me." The spirit behind white supremacy is not of God—it is a spiritual deception rooted in hierarchy, violence, and idolatry. America, much like ancient Aryan societies, has idolized monuments and symbols of conquest, treating them as divine while erasing the stories of those they oppressed.

The prophet Isaiah spoke to this deception:

"For your hands are defiled with blood...They hatch vipers' eggs and weave the spider's web; he who eats of their eggs dies."

(Isaiah 59:3-5)

When Europeans arrived in Africa, they encountered advanced, thriving civilizations. Yet they wielded a weaponized form of

Christianity to control and colonize. Many African leaders accepted this foreign faith without realizing its distortion. Once the breadbasket of Rome and the world, Africa was robbed of its wealth, resources, and dignity.

With every slave ship, Africa lost not only people but crops, gold, and culture. In exchange, Europeans brought division, self-hatred, and spiritual confusion. The prophets had warned of this betrayal. Ezekiel spoke of being handed over to those once despised (Ezekiel 23:16-30). Jeremiah called for repentance, not to flee. But the enslavers—descendants of Indo-European tribes from the Balkans—carried out their assault in the name of civilization.

To maintain their dominance, colonizers severed Africans from their God and heritage. Supremacy thrived when spiritual loyalty was redirected to myths of white rule. As Deuteronomy warned:

*"The Lord will change the rain of your land to powder and dust...
you shall become troublesome to all the kingdoms of the earth."*

(Deut. 28:24-25)

This was not just about land or labor—it was a spiritual war against a people and their divine covenant. Africa's wealth was extracted. Its people are scattered. Its culture attacked. And all of it was cloaked in a lie: that white power was ordained by God. But the truth, hidden in plain sight, cries out for justice, accountability, and a return to righteousness.

The Dutch arrived in Africa during the 1600s, establishing a supply station in what is now Cape Town to support their voyages between Europe and Asia. By 1652, they began building settlements along the southern coast of Africa, taking land and resources from Indigenous peoples. These colonial settlements marked the beginning of brutal oppression for many Africans. Over the next fifty years, the Dutch became a dominant colonial power in both Africa and the Americas.

The Struggle for Africa's Wealth and Power

Although the British briefly took control of South Africa in 1795, the Dutch remained economically and politically stronger than Portugal and were among Europe's wealthiest merchant powers. Initially drawn to Africa for gold, they soon challenged Portugal and France for dominance of the West African coast.

The Dutch seized several Portuguese forts, including Elmina Castle in present-day Ghana, and expanded plantation slavery. As European appetite for sugar and other crops exploded, so did the demand for African labor. The Dutch became deeply invested in the transatlantic slave trade, turning human lives into commodities to fuel European economies.

Their shipbuilding industry grew into the largest in the world, carrying half of Europe's maritime cargo. Gold and silver flowed from Africa and the Americas into European treasuries, enriching colonial powers while devastating Indigenous and African societies.

In 1609, the Dutch founded New Netherland along the Hudson River, laying the foundation for present-day New York, New Jersey, Delaware, and Staten Island. Just a decade later, in 1619, the first African captives arrived in the British colony of Virginia aboard a Dutch ship, marking the beginning of racialized slavery in what would become the United States.

By 1624, the Dutch West India Company had established a colony in Manhattan and became fierce rivals with England and France. Their colonies relied on enslaved Africans to resolve labor shortages and amass wealth.

In 1652, the Dutch East India Company established a permanent settlement at the Cape of Good Hope. This station became a hub for ships moving between Europe, Africa, and the Americas. But as Dutch settlements expanded, many Indigenous Africans fled inland, while others were violently displaced.

The Dutch launched military campaigns to remove Indigenous groups like the San (Bushmen) and Khoikhoi from their land, often enslaving those they captured. These groups, made up of hunter-gatherers and herders, were nearly wiped out by Dutch violence and forced removals. As colonists expanded further, they encountered resistance from the Zulu.

The British seized the Cape Colony in 1806, pushing tribes off their land. In response, King Shaka of the Zulu united neighboring tribes and built a powerful army. Though Zulu forces scored a major victory in 1879 at the Battle of Isandlwana—killing 2,000 British soldiers—the British regrouped and eventually crushed the Zulu resistance.

In 1866, massive diamond reserves were discovered near the Orange River in present-day Kimberly. The "Big Hole" mine alone produced over three tons of diamonds, giving rise to powerful companies like De Beers. By 1886, gold was found in Gauteng Province (Witwatersrand), leading to the rise of Johannesburg.

These discoveries fueled new waves of colonial greed. The British seized control of diamond and gold-rich regions, sparking conflict with the Dutch. Eventually, Britain claimed dominance over South Africa's most lucrative resources, including the Gold Coast of Ghana.

In The Power of Gold, historian Peter L. Bernstein writes: "In order to extract South Africa's annual output of around five hundred tons of gold, some seventy million tons of earth must be raised and milled—an amount greater than all the material in the pyramid of Cheops."

This industrial-scale extraction enriched European empires while leaving African communities displaced, exploited, and stripped of their ancestral lands. The legacy of that exploitation lives on in today's global inequality, racial hierarchies, and ongoing struggles for justice in post-colonial nations.

In the 1800s, the British launched military campaigns to claim vast territories in southern Africa, including present-day Johannesburg, Transvaal, the Orange Free State, and Natal. These conquests required massive labor forces, especially for the expanding mining industry. Though Britain officially outlawed the transatlantic slave trade in 1807, it continued to build the largest colonial empire on the African continent.

To settle disputes over Africa's division, German Chancellor Otto von Bismarck convened the Berlin Conference in 1884–1885. European powers—Britain, France, Germany, Belgium, Italy, Spain, and Portugal—gathered to partition the continent without African representation. By 1914, nearly all of Africa was under European control, except Ethiopia and Liberia.

White settlers flooded the continent, extracting Africa's natural wealth—diamonds, gold, copper, rubber, ivory, timber—while forcing Indigenous communities off their land.

They constructed infrastructure for their benefit, creating whites-only schools, hospitals, parks, and beaches. Across the continent, resistance by Africans was met with brutal violence. Women and children suffered alongside men, and any protest was met with bullets from colonial troops.

Black Africans were oppressed through forced labor systems, toiling under inhumane conditions to benefit white settlers. Of all the colonial powers, Britain inherited the most territory, emerging as the largest empire, following the legacy of Rome.

"Here is the mind which has wisdom: The seven heads are seven mountains on which the woman sits. There are also seven kings. Five have fallen, one is, and the other has not yet come. And when he comes, he must continue a short time."

(Revelation 17:9–10)

Amid white colonial domination, resistance movements began to emerge. In South Africa, Nehemiah Tile helped found the Tembu National Church and the Ethiopian Church of South Africa—African-led Christian movements rejecting racial hierarchies and white supremacy. These independent churches linked faith to liberation, restoring dignity, cultural pride, and education to Black communities.

In 1885, Italy invaded Eritrea and later attempted to colonize Ethiopia. However, at the Battle of Adwa in 1896, Ethiopian Emperor Menelik II led 100,000 troops to victory against 20,000 Italian soldiers, killing nearly 2,000. Ethiopia became the only African nation to successfully repel European colonization. European powers retaliated by attacking Ethiopia's trade partners, trying to weaken its economy.

"The beast that was, and is not, is himself also the eighth, and is of the seven, and is going to perdition."

(Revelation 17:11)

Meanwhile, in the 18th century, British colonial rule in North America sparked rebellion. After defeating France in a seven-year war, Britain imposed strict tax policies and trade restrictions on its 13 colonies. The colonies—rich with enslaved labor and agricultural expertise—resisted, leading to the American Revolution and the birth of the United States.

While the U.S. was founded on cries of liberty, its economy depended on slavery. Both Black and white colonists opposed British rule. One of the first to die in protest was Crispus Attucks, a formerly enslaved Black man killed during the Boston Massacre of 1770, becoming an early martyr in the struggle for independence.

These events reveal how systemic racism and white supremacy were embedded in both colonial conquests abroad and the founding of modern Western nations. The myths of freedom and progress were often built on stolen land, stolen labor, and the suppression of Black and Indigenous peoples.

In 1763, after the Seven Years' War, Britain attempted to tighten control over its American colonies by imposing a series of unpopular taxes to repay its war debt. Parliament believed the colonies should help fund the empire that had protected them. In 1765, they passed the Stamp Act, which required tax stamps on legal documents, newspapers, playing cards, and more. This triggered widespread outrage among the colonists and sparked the rallying cry: "No taxation without representation."

By April 1775, the American Revolutionary War began at Lexington and Concord. The 13 colonies had begun seizing local governments and pushing out British officials. The Patriots—Black and white alike—fought for freedom and self-determination. Nearly half of the colonists, however, remained loyal to Britain. These Loyalists, often from wealthier, elite circles, feared that independence would mean economic instability and mob rule. Many were attacked or exiled for their allegiance.

Most Native American nations sided with the British, believing a British victory would halt settler expansion. The Iroquois Confederacy, one of the most powerful Indigenous alliances, split during the war. While they had once united under Deganawida's vision of peace and trade, they now found themselves caught between two colonial powers. Indigenous warriors used their deep knowledge of the land to attack colonial forts, burn settlements, and capture American soldiers. Some tribes, fed up with deceitful British trade practices, sided with the colonists, seeking revenge.

African Americans also played a crucial role. At the war's outset, both free and enslaved Black men fought bravely in early battles like Lexington, Concord, and Bunker Hill. But in July 1775, General George Washington took control of the Continental Army and banned Black enlistment, refusing to offer freedom in exchange for service.

This decision backfired. When the war shifted to New York and the colonies suffered devastating defeats, Britain saw an opportunity. The British promised freedom to enslaved people who joined their forces. Thousands of Black men fled southern colonies like Georgia and the Carolinas to fight for Britain.

Some were later returned to their enslavers or executed for fleeing.

The bravery of Black soldiers did not go unnoticed. Rhode Island broke ranks with Washington's policy and began recruiting Black troops. By 1777, Washington reversed course with the war turning against the colonies. He finally allowed Black soldiers— free or enslaved—to fight for the Continental Army, offering freedom in return. It was a reluctant but necessary concession that revealed how Black liberation was only considered when it benefited the survival of white-led rebellion.

The Racialized Birth of America's Freedom

This chapter in American history reminds us that the struggle for freedom has always been racialized. African Americans fought for a liberty that wasn't promised to them. Indigenous communities defended their homelands against two colonizing powers. And systemic injustice was baked into the very foundations of the American republic.

On July 2, 1776, all 13 American colonies met in Philadelphia to vote on independence from British rule. Two days later, on July 4, the United States Declaration of Independence was formally adopted, declaring the colonies a sovereign nation.

Following this declaration, Spain, France, and later the Netherlands joined the conflict, offering crucial support to the colonists against Britain. France signed treaties to back the revolution until the colonies won their independence. Despite this growing support, American troops faced setbacks. On May 12, 1780, 5,000 American soldiers surrendered in Charleston, South Carolina.

Still, the colonists held firm. At Bunker Hill, although the British eventually took the position, they suffered over 1,100 casualties, making it one of the bloodiest battles of the war. The tide turned for good in Yorktown, Virginia, where the British army surrendered on October 19, 1781. A peace treaty was ratified by the Continental Congress on April 19, 1783, ending the war.

The rise of the United States mirrored the trajectory of Rome: from a small colony to a global superpower. Just as Rome expanded from a tiny Greek-influenced city into an empire, America grew from 13 colonies into the most influential power since Adam ceded dominion of the Garden of Eden. Some have drawn comparisons between America and the prophetic "Mystery Babylon" described in scripture.

The United States promised liberty, equality, and the pursuit of happiness, but failed to extend those rights to all. During the Civil War, free Black Americans and enslaved Africans were promised freedom for their service, but most were returned to slavery after the fighting ended. Even those who fought bravely were betrayed by a system never designed to include them.

This exclusion was no accident—it was foundational. America, like Rome, built its dominance through exploitation, systemic racism, and a caste structure rooted in white supremacy. Many today still deny this, blaming Black communities for their own oppression instead of acknowledging the legacy of slavery, segregation, and inequality that shaped the nation's wealth and power.

Black people were indispensable to the birth of America. From agriculture to battlefield contributions, they were at the heart of the country's success. But their sacrifices were never properly recognized, and the promises made to them were broken.

Racism, like a spiritual disease, justified cruelty, violence, and the theft of land and labor. America inherited the structural racism of Europe and amplified it. Rome's downfall came from external enemies and its failure to deal with internal inequality and injustice. America, too, faces a reckoning.

The foundational ideals of liberty and justice remain powerful but have never been fully realized. Until America confronts its legacy of systemic racism and caste oppression, it will remain haunted by the contradictions on which it was built.

Many of America's foundational government structures were built by enslaved labor and modeled after the Roman Empire. Yet despite emancipation and constitutional promises, the wealth gap between white and Black Americans remains staggering. Today, the average white household holds nearly ten times the wealth of the average Black household, regardless of education level. Centuries of systemic racism, economic exclusion, and white privilege have prevented Black families from achieving lasting economic security.

More than 150 years after slavery's abolition, protests continue to expose the profound racial injustice woven into America's systems. Black neighborhoods remain over-policed, underfunded, and systematically excluded from equal access to healthcare, homeownership, employment, and capital. For many, the promise of liberty has been delayed or denied.

The American caste system mirrors the Hindu caste structure in India, both enforcing racialized hierarchies that favor whiteness and marginalize Black and brown people. America's roots trace back to European settlers—descendants of Indo-Aryans who, thousands of years earlier, invaded and imposed caste-based rule over Indigenous populations in India. Those same ideologies crossed the Atlantic with Anglo-Saxon settlers who justified dominance as divinely ordained.

When the pilgrims landed in Plymouth, Massachusetts, the Native people welcomed them and taught them survival skills. Their cooperation led to the first Thanksgiving. But as the colonists' population and profits grew, so did their greed for land. They expanded aggressively, seized Indigenous territories, and launched attacks, capturing Native women and children, burning crops, and labeling Natives as animals.

After the Revolutionary War, Native peoples across the Southeast and Midwest were forcibly removed from their homelands and relocated to government-controlled reservations. Many Cherokees, Choctaws, and Seminoles resisted, retreating to places like the Florida Everglades. Their resistance—and their refusal to return runaway Black slaves—triggered the Seminole Wars under General Andrew Jackson, who became the first governor of Florida.

In the aftermath of U.S. expansion and the discovery of gold in Minnesota, tribes such as the Sioux and Cheyenne were pushed into Oklahoma. A particularly gruesome chapter unfolded in 1864, when the Third Colorado Cavalry massacred peaceful Cheyenne villagers at Sand Creek. Chiefs Black Kettle and Antelope had negotiated a treaty for U.S. protection, only to be betrayed.

Governor John Evans ordered Colonel John Chivington—a former preacher—to remove the Natives by force. On November

29, Chivington's troops surrounded the camp at night and launched a brutal assault. Under orders to take no prisoners, soldiers slaughtered women and children, mutilated the dead, and displayed their scalps. Chief Antelope was tortured and dismembered in a grotesque act of racial violence.

This was not an isolated event, but a reflection of the broader pattern of white supremacy, land theft, and genocidal violence that defined U.S. expansion. These atrocities—and the system that enabled them—must be remembered not as distant history, but as part of the ongoing struggle for truth, justice, and reparations.

Haiti's Revolution and Its Impact on Abolition

During the Abolitionist Movement in America, activists became the leading voices against the horrors of slavery, racial oppression, and systemic injustice. In the Southern states, enslaved Black people were deliberately kept illiterate—reading or writing could lead to brutal punishments, from beatings to mutilation.

Still, many risked their lives to learn. Literacy became a path to freedom and resistance, challenging the power structure that depended on silence and submission. 1817 the American Colonization Society emerged, promoting sending free Black people to Liberia or Sierra Leone. Though framed as a peaceful "solution," it was rooted in white fear—an effort to remove Black people rather than confront racism.

While Britain had already established Sierra Leone in 1787 as a home for formerly enslaved Africans, the U.S. version of this movement never earned widespread support among abolitionists. Many free Black Americans—born and raised in the U.S.—saw this country as their rightful home. The colonization effort only reinforced the lie that Black people could never coexist with whites as equals.

Paul Cuffee, a wealthy shipowner of African and Indigenous descent, supported a return to Africa and helped finance voyages. His vision helped send more than 11,000 formerly enslaved people to West Africa, with Liberia becoming an independent republic in 1847. But for most abolitionists, the goal wasn't exile—it was justice, equality, and the complete dismantling of slavery.

As abolitionist efforts expanded, resistance grew more radical. People were no longer afraid to fight for their freedom. One of the earliest large-scale uprisings was the 1739 Stono Rebellion in South Carolina, led by an African-born man named Jemmy. Chanting "Liberty," he and his followers killed several white slaveholders and freed others before being brutally crushed.

Perhaps the most well-known revolt was led by Nat Turner, a preacher and visionary who believed he was called by God to lead his people out of bondage. His 1831 rebellion resulted in the deaths of about 60 white slaveholders and their families, while sparing poor whites. Turner's uprising terrified the white establishment and was viewed as a rebellion not just against slavery, but against the racial order itself. In their eyes, it was defiance against God, though they used religion to justify centuries of theft, terror, and dehumanization.

In response to growing unrest, the Abolitionist Movement used media—newspapers, poems, essays, and personal narratives—to expose the horrors of slavery. These firsthand accounts became powerful tools to awaken the conscience of the public.

William Lloyd Garrison, a white Christian abolitionist, launched The Liberator, declaring slavery "a covenant with death," and condemning the U.S. Constitution for enabling it.

His words echoed the prophet Isaiah, calling oppression "a covenant with death". Elijah P. Lovejoy, another abolitionist minister, was murdered by a white mob for defending a Black man in the press. His death symbolized how violently white supremacy responded to truth-telling.

Despite the danger, abolitionists—both Black and white— turned their homes into safe havens on the Underground Railroad. They challenged the system, not with weapons alone, but with the power of solidarity, justice, and unwavering conviction.

In 1804, Haiti declared its independence, abolishing slavery and becoming the first Black republic in the Western Hemisphere. The success of the Haitian Revolution sent shockwaves through the Americas and terrified white slaveholding societies. Its influence rippled into the northern U.S., where states began moving toward abolition.

The United Kingdom banned the Atlantic slave trade in 1807 and took steps to stop slave ships leaving Africa. Meanwhile, the U.S. lagged, clinging to racial hierarchy, white fear, and the systemic exploitation of Black bodies.

The Civil War tore the United States apart politically, socially, and spiritually. It fractured families and exposed deep divisions, not only between the North and South but also within the Abolitionist Movement itself. Some abolitionists remained idealistic and focused on gradual change, while others believed slavery was a moral abomination—"an agreement with hell"—that required urgent, radical action.

At the center of this radical movement was John Brown, a white Christian abolitionist who believed slavery was so evil that only direct, armed resistance could destroy it. In 1859, Brown led a daring raid on a federal armory in Harper's Ferry, Virginia, with the goal of starting a massive slave uprising. Though the raid ultimately failed, Brown's actions—and his willingness to die for the cause—shook the conscience of the nation.

Brown's passion for justice had deep roots. His father, Owen Brown, supported the Underground Railroad and taught his son that God would one day punish America for slavery. John Brown took that belief to heart. Before the Harper's Ferry raid, he had already taken part in violent retaliation against pro-slavery forces who had burned abolitionist newspapers. He attacked the free-state town of Lawrence, Kansas.

In what became known as the Pottawatomie Massacre, Brown and his followers killed five pro-slavery men. It was a bloody signal that the fight over slavery would no longer be waged only with words.

When Brown and his group seized the armory at Harper's Ferry, they hoped to arm enslaved people across the South. But support didn't come as expected. Although they freed about 30 enslaved people and captured a relative of George Washington, Brown and his small band were quickly surrounded. U.S. Marines, led by Robert E. Lee, were sent to crush the rebellion. Brown's sons were killed in the attack, and he was captured.

John Brown was tried for treason and executed. But in death, he became a martyr for freedom. His final words before his hanging were a chilling prophecy:

"If it is deemed necessary that I should forfeit my life for the furtherance of justice... let it be done."

His actions and words had a profound effect on the North. For many Black activists and abolitionists, Brown became a symbol of white allyship grounded in action, not just belief.

Once skeptical of Brown's violent methods, Frederick Douglass came to deeply admire him. In an 1882 speech at Harper's Ferry, Douglass declared:

"His zeal in the cause of freedom was infinitely superior to mine. Mine was a tapered light; his was the burning sun... I could speak for the enslaved person. John Brown could fight for the enslaved people. I could live as an enslaved person. John Brown could die for the enslaved person."

Lincoln and the End of Slavery

In November 1860, Abraham Lincoln was elected president with just 40% of the popular vote and no support from the Southern states. Southern leaders immediately viewed him as a threat, fearing he would interfere with their economic dependence on slavery, even though Lincoln had never explicitly called for its immediate abolition. He believed the federal government had no authority to end slavery in states where it already existed, but he strongly opposed its expansion into new territories.

This tension between federal power and states' rights exposed deeper divisions within the country. Southern states, feeling politically unrepresented and economically vulnerable, began seceding from the Union, forming the Confederate States of America. Lincoln and the Republican Party campaigned against the spread of slavery, while the South insisted that maintaining slavery was essential to their survival and identity.

Lincoln recognized that slavery was at the heart of America's divide, famously warning that "a house divided against itself cannot stand." Yet, at the start of the Civil War, Lincoln's priority was preserving the Union, not freeing the enslaved. Even after taking office in March 1861, he initially returned escaped enslaved people to their Southern enslavers, which sparked criticism from abolitionists who pushed him to name slavery as the root cause of the conflict.

By April 1861, the war officially began when Confederate forces attacked Fort Sumter in South Carolina. The Confederacy hoped for support from Britain and France, who relied on Southern cotton. However, Charles Francis Adams, son of John Quincy Adams, persuaded Britain not to recognize the Confederacy, keeping European powers out of the war.

As the war escalated, German immigrants, many of whom had fled persecution in Europe, formed a key bloc within the abolitionist cause. Their engineering, logistics, and communication skills helped modernize the Union war effort, contributing to its use of railroads, steamships, and telegraphs to gain a technological edge over the South.

In places like Texas, resistance to Confederate authority grew. German Americans who opposed slavery and refused to be drafted fled toward Mexico, but many were ambushed and massacred by Confederate soldiers in what became known as the Nueces Massacre.

By the second year of war, with heavy losses mounting on both sides—including over 12,000 Union soldiers at Antietam—Lincoln faced mounting pressure to shift the war's moral focus. He issued the Emancipation Proclamation, declaring that if the Southern states didn't rejoin the Union by January 1, 1863, all enslaved people in Confederate territories would be declared free.

As the Civil War dragged on and casualties mounted on both sides, President Abraham Lincoln issued the Emancipation Proclamation on September 22, 1862, declaring that all enslaved people in Confederate-controlled territories would be free as of January 1, 1863. However, this declaration did not apply to enslaved people in Union-held states, revealing Lincoln's moral commitment limits. It was a strategic political move designed to weaken the Southern economy, not necessarily to affirm Black humanity.

In reality, slavery was still allowed in states that remained loyal to the Union, exposing the hypocrisy and convenience of white power structures. Black lives were leveraged as pawns in a larger struggle for control, not justice. While some saw emancipation as a step toward liberation, for many enslaved people, it was too little, too late. They had already begun freeing themselves—fleeing plantations, joining Union lines, and resisting their oppressors on their terms.

Southern slaveholders feared that once freed, Black people would rise and seek revenge for centuries of brutality. This fear fueled even harsher repression. Those who tried to escape were often captured, tortured, or killed. Yet thousands of formerly enslaved people joined the Union Army, not just to fight the Confederacy but to fight for their liberation.

Black soldiers became critical to the Union's success, serving as scouts, soldiers, and laborers, bringing intimate knowledge of the Southern landscape. Despite unequal treatment, they fought with unmatched courage and sacrifice. Over 35,000 Black soldiers died in the war, and 23 were awarded the Medal of Honor. Meanwhile, the war itself claimed over 620,000 lives, making it the bloodiest conflict in U.S. history.

While many white Northerners framed the war as a noble fight to preserve the Union, Black people understood the deeper stakes. This was not just a war between regions—it was a war for the soul of the nation, a reckoning with its original sin: slavery.

Finally, on February 1, 1865, Lincoln signed the Thirteenth Amendment, officially abolishing slavery. It was ratified on December 18, 1865, ending legalized slavery across the United States. But freedom on paper did not mean true liberation. The systems of racial hierarchy, rooted in the same caste logic that defined both Hindu and American societies, did not disappear with emancipation. They evolved, morphing into new forms of systemic oppression that persist today.

Like Julius Caesar crossing the Rubicon and plunging Rome into civil war, America had reached the point of no return. The war had been fought. The blood had been spilled. But the real struggle—freedom, equality, and justice for all—was far from over.

CHAPTER 11

Freedom Contested and Power Redefined

After the Civil War, the Reconstruction era marked a brief but powerful moment when African Americans made historic gains. Formerly enslaved people owned land, opened businesses, voted, and held political office. Seventeen Black men were elected to the U.S. Congress. For the first time, America seemed to be inching toward its promise of liberty and justice for all.

In March 1865, Congress created the Freedmen's Bureau to help newly freed Black people and poor whites with basic needs like food, education, and healthcare services that had been systematically denied to enslaved people. President Abraham Lincoln had also proposed redistributing land in

40-acre plots to freedmen, but his assassination ended that possibility. In 1867, Congressman Thaddeus Stevens pushed for the confiscation of Southern plantations to give Black families real independence, but the bill never passed.

Instead, sharecropping became the norm. Landowners let Black farmers use land in exchange for half the harvest. In theory, this gave formerly enslaved people independence. In practice, it was a new form of economic bondage designed to trap Black families in cycles of poverty. White privilege evolved not through chains but through contracts.

The desire to reimpose racial hierarchy remained strong. Many white Americans saw true Black freedom as a threat. Apartheid in America wasn't formalized like South Africa's, but it was no less real—it was embedded in every institution, from birth to death.

Radical Republicans in Congress tried to protect Black civil rights, pushing federal legislation over state control. In 1866, Congress passed the Civil Rights Act, overriding President Andrew Johnson's veto and expanding the powers of the Freedmen's Bureau. The act declared that Black people were citizens and deserved equal protection under the law—a radical shift in a nation built on slavery.

1868 the 14th Amendment was ratified, affirming that all people born or naturalized in the U.S.—regardless of race— were full citizens. In 1870, the 15th Amendment made denying the right to vote based on race was illegal. But these legal protections were met with rage in the South, where Black political power began to rise, especially in states like South Carolina, where the Black population was the majority.

That progress sparked violent backlash. In 1866, Nathan Bedford Forrest, a former Confederate general and slave trader, co-founded the Ku Klux Klan in Pulaski, Tennessee. This white supremacist group used terrorism—lynchings, arson, beatings—to stop Black people from voting, learning, organizing, or dreaming of equality. They targeted schools, churches, and Freedmen's Bureau offices, trying to destroy every institution that empowered Black communities.

The Klan wasn't just a fringe group—it became part of the mainstream. Its members infiltrated law enforcement, the courts, and government. With the withdrawal of federal troops from the South in 1877, the brief window of Black empowerment closed. Jim Crow laws swept in, establishing a legal caste system in America.

These laws weren't just about "separate but equal"—they were about preserving white supremacy through state-sanctioned oppression. The very rights gained during Reconstruction were slowly dismantled through legal loopholes, violence, and silence.

White Supremacy After Slavery

Between 1860 and 1920, over 5,000 Black people were lynched across the United States. Many white allies were also murdered for standing in solidarity. These lynchings were more than acts of violence—they were public messages, meant to enforce white supremacy and punish any sign of Black progress.

Jim Crow laws were created to block African American advancement and reestablish white control after the gains of Reconstruction. These laws prohibited Black people from working in many professions, owning property, or participating in civic life. White society used legal and social tools to return Black people to a condition that closely resembled slavery.

The Black Codes, passed shortly after the Civil War, criminalized freedom. Under Vagrancy Laws, Black men between 18 and 60 had to carry proof of employment or face arrest. If they couldn't pay the fines, they were "hired out" to white employers—slavery by another name. Black people were also barred from traveling, attending white schools, entering public parks, and staying in hotels. Even simple acts, like using a front door instead of the back, were met with hostility and violence.

President Andrew Johnson, a Tennessee Democrat who took office after Lincoln's assassination, openly opposed Black citizenship. He vetoed key bills designed to protect freedmen, arguing that the federal government should not feed, clothe, or educate ex-slaves. To many white Southerners, Black progress felt like it was moving too fast. The Black Codes were designed to slow it down, reassert control, and undermine every gain of emancipation.

White landowners seized Black property, and those who resisted were often lynched, burned alive, or dragged from their homes by mobs. The Ku Klux Klan—formed by former Confederate soldiers in 1866—used terrorism to keep Black people from voting, learning, or organizing. Cross burnings, mob attacks, and murders became tools of intimidation. Even Black success stories were met with violence.

1877 after a contested election, Rutherford B. Hayes became president despite losing the popular vote. He had promised to protect Black civil rights, but instead ended Reconstruction, withdrawing federal troops from the South. With the military gone, white supremacists regained control, and the progress of the past decade collapsed almost overnight.

Polling places became dangerous. White mobs assassinated political leaders, disrupted meetings, and killed Black citizens trying to vote or organize. Ministers preached sermons glorifying the Klan, and images of Black bodies hanging from trees became symbols of white power.

Meanwhile, federal institutions failed to act. Many white law enforcement officers, judges, and elected officials ignored civil rights violations. In 1857, before the war, the infamous Dred Scott decision declared that Black people were "beings of an inferior order" with no rights that the white man was bound to respect. That mindset lived on long after slavery ended.

Even the Supreme Court upheld segregation, legalizing a racial caste system that resembled the varna system of Hindu India, where one's status was inherited and unchangeable. The American caste system used whiteness as a badge of dominance and Blackness as a justification for exclusion, violence, and labor exploitation.

When Black people tried to escape this oppression by land, sea, or train, white mobs blocked their migration, threatening violence. The South needed Black labor, but refused to offer dignity, freedom, or equal treatment.

This period exposed a deeper truth: the end of slavery did not mean the end of oppression. It simply evolved, repackaged through laws, institutions, and cultural narratives, reinforcing a system of white supremacy that is still with us today.

Black Resistance and White Terror

After the death of his enslaver, Dr. John Emerson, Dred Scott lived in the free Wisconsin Territory for a time. Although Emerson's widow abandoned him, she refused to grant him legal freedom. Scott lived with Henry Blow, a white abolitionist who supported his legal fight for emancipation. But the Supreme Court ruled that the rights and privileges of the Constitution applied only to white citizens, solidifying the idea that Black people—enslaved or free—had no legal standing in America. The court also upheld bans on interracial marriage, reinforcing white racial purity as a pillar of American law.

In the early 1900s, as tensions rose between European nations, African Americans used the moment to press for human rights. Many migrated to the north in search of better opportunities, but structural racism followed them. Though jobs were more available, Black migrants were often denied education and skilled labor positions, locking them into poverty.

To help with the transition to urban life, the National Urban League was founded in New York City in 1910. A year earlier, the NAACP had been established by W.E.B. Du Bois and members of the Niagara Movement, along with white allies. These groups fought for civil rights through protests, legal challenges, and voter registration. Du Bois helped expand the global scope of the movement, organizing the Second Pan-African Congress and linking African American liberation to a broader global struggle.

In the 1920s and 1930s, the Harlem Renaissance exploded onto the cultural scene. This movement blended politics, music, theater, art, and literature into a powerful statement of Black identity and brilliance. Harlem became a beacon of Black pride and creativity, challenging white stereotypes and redefining what it meant to be African American.

Ironically, Harlem's nightlife attracted white patrons from Manhattan, eager to enjoy Black talent while still denying Black people basic rights. Yet for many African Americans, this was a time to embrace their true African heritage, reclaim dignity, and resist invisibility.

Alongside these cultural awakenings, various Black Hebrew organizations emerged, spiritually identifying African Americans as descendants of the ancient Israelites. These movements challenged the erasure of Black history and connected Black people to their biblical identity.

Meanwhile, the one-drop rule, rooted in Jim Crow ideology, legally defined anyone with a trace of African ancestry as Black. This racist classification sought to protect white racial purity at all costs. The fear that a white person might unknowingly have "Black blood" reflected the deep anxiety of a system built on lies and denial. The hypocrisy ran deep—white men had long abused enslaved Black women and fathered biracial children without consequence, yet denied those children equality or recognition.

Black blood was spilled across the nation—not for what people had done, but simply for who they were. Systemic racism, economic exclusion, and humiliation followed every effort by Black communities to rise. Jim Crow was not just segregation—it was a racial caste system, designed to keep Black people "in their place."

After World War I, many Black veterans returned home,

hoping their service would earn them equality. Instead, they were met with continued discrimination. But this time, they organized. Black leaders, business owners, and everyday people began boycotting stores that refused to hire Black workers and standing up against unjust hiring practices. They demanded economic justice and respect.

In the South, these protests were often met with Confederate flags and racial hostility. But they also sparked a new wave of awareness—one that inspired diverse communities to question the myth of white supremacy. The push for civil rights, born of centuries of struggle, began to reshape the soul of the nation.

Despite the end of slavery, many white Americans continued to view Black people as inferior and in need of control. Vigilante groups like the Ku Klux Klan (KKK) grew in power, presenting themselves as guardians of "order" while unleashing terror on Black communities. Any sign of Black progress—whether economic, political, or social—was met with violence, intimidation, and retaliation.

Interracial relationships were criminalized, and even a rumor could lead to beatings, imprisonment, or lynching. In the 1920s, public lynchings were often treated like community events, drawing crowds of white men, women, and children. Black people were whipped, burned, or hanged in full view of cheering mobs. Law enforcement often participated or looked the other way, and local papers even advertised upcoming lynchings. This culture of impunity fueled white supremacy and legitimized racial terror.

In the South, uniformed Klansmen stormed Black-owned businesses, demanding they be sold or abandoned. Blacks were denied the right to testify in court against white people. White politicians openly defended these atrocities, while symbols like nooses and burning crosses became tools of racial intimidation.

One of the worst acts of racial violence in U.S. history occurred in Tulsa, Oklahoma, in 1921, targeting the thriving Black community of Greenwood, often called Black Wall Street.

On May 30, 1921, a 19-year-old Black shoe shiner named Dick Rowland entered the Drexel Building to use the elevator. Inside was Sara Page, a 17-year-old white elevator operator. When the elevator jolted, Rowland accidentally stumbled against Page. She screamed, and Rowland fled. The next day, he was arrested and falsely accused of attempted assault. Although Page later dropped the charges, it was too late—a white mob had already formed.

Black World War I veterans and community leaders, knowing the threat of lynching was real, went to the courthouse to protect Rowland. A white man tried to grab a Black veteran's gun, and a shot was fired. Chaos erupted, and the mob retaliated with violence that would soon destroy an entire community.

By morning, thousands of armed white men, including many deputized Klansmen, launched a full assault on Greenwood. Black residents were pulled from their homes, businesses were looted, and churches, hospitals, hotels, and schools were set on fire. Planes flew overhead, dropping dynamite on homes. Around 6,000 Black residents were forced at gunpoint into detention centers, and an estimated 300 people were killed, although exact numbers were never officially recorded.

The Roots of Greenwood and Black Prosperity in Oklahoma. After the Civil War, Indigenous Territory became a refuge for African Americans fleeing racial violence and economic exploitation in the Deep South. Between 1865 and 1920, more than 50 Black townships were established in what would become Oklahoma—driven by the hope for land, safety, and self-determination.

A major turning point came with the Dawes Act of 1887. This federal law divided tribal lands into individual plots— including for Black members of Native tribes—opening the door for African Americans to acquire property and build independent communities. But while it offered opportunity, it also marked the beginning of federal interference, surveillance, and the erosion of tribal sovereignty and Black progress.

O.W. Gurley: Building Black Wall Street. Ottowa W. Gurley, a visionary Black entrepreneur, played a key role in Greenwood's rise. Born to formerly enslaved parents in Alabama and raised in Arkansas, Gurley arrived in Oklahoma during the 1889 Land Rush. After running a general store in Perry, he moved to oil-rich Tulsa and reportedly purchased 40 acres on the city's north side. His goal was clear: to create a self-sufficient Black community.

Gurley opened a rooming house, acquired more properties, and gave loans to other Black families and business owners. His investments laid the foundation for what would become known as "Black Wall Street"—a thriving, independent district built by and for Black people.

J.B. Stradford: Power and Persecution. Another pillar of Greenwood was J.B. Stradford, a lawyer and entrepreneur born in Kentucky to a formerly enslaved father. Before moving to Tulsa in 1899, Stradford had already built wealth through boarding houses and businesses. He soon invested heavily in Greenwood, eventually building the Stradford Hotel—the largest Black-owned hotel in the country. With over 50 luxury suites, a saloon, and live jazz, the hotel became a cornerstone of Greenwood's vibrant middle class.

But Black success drew white resentment. After a white mob terrorized the district in the 1921 Tulsa Race Massacre, Stradford was scapegoated and falsely charged with inciting a riot. His real "crime" was helping build Black prosperity. Facing execution or life in prison, he fled to Kansas and later settled in Chicago.

Greenwood Wasn't an Exception—It Was a Threat. What happened in Tulsa wasn't an accident or isolated act of violence—it was part of a larger pattern of racial terrorism across the United States. Greenwood's success was seen as dangerous because it disproved the myth of Black inferiority. It showed what Black communities could achieve when left to thrive on their own terms. That is precisely what white supremacy could not tolerate.

Greenwood is a symbol—not just of Black excellence, but also of the fear it sparked in a society built on racial hierarchy. And today, as we confront ongoing efforts to silence Black history and dismantle equity programs, we must remember Greenwood's lesson: true justice requires truth, memory, and repair.

CHAPTER 12

Civil Rights Era

By 1936, Black Americans began shifting political support from the Republican Party to Franklin D. Roosevelt, whose New Deal programs offered hope during the Great Depression. Roosevelt's administration became the first to include civil rights in a national conversation. In 1941, he issued an executive order establishing the Fair Employment Practices Committee (FEPC), banning workplace discrimination based on race, religion, color, or national origin. He also helped 50,000 Black farmers access government loans and introduced a federal minimum wage—critical steps toward economic inclusion.

First Lady Eleanor Roosevelt also used her position to fight racism. Eleanor resigned when the Daughters of the American

Revolution (DAR) refused to let world-renowned Black opera singer Marian Anderson perform at Constitution Hall. She helped organize Anderson's now-legendary performance on the steps of the Lincoln Memorial—an act of protest witnessed by over 75,000 people.

After Roosevelt's death in 1945, Vice President Harry S. Truman became president. Though he had once admitted to holding racist views, Truman was moved by the brutal treatment of Black WWII veterans and became the first president to address the NAACP. He openly condemned Jim Crow laws, poll taxes, and racial terrorism. Truman's efforts to dismantle white supremacy angered many Southern Democrats, who broke away and became known as Dixiecrats.

Truman also pushed for laws to prosecute the Ku Klux Klan and end racial violence, challenging the idea that "states' rights" could be used to protect hate groups.

In 1957, a young pastor named Dr. Martin Luther King Jr. helped form the Southern Christian Leadership Conference (SCLC) to organize nonviolent protests for civil rights. King, then minister of Dexter Avenue Baptist Church in Montgomery, Alabama, was inspired to act after Rosa Parks, a seamstress and NAACP secretary, was arrested for refusing to give up her bus seat to a white passenger.

The Montgomery Bus Boycott, organized by the Montgomery Improvement Association, lasted 381 days. Dr. King was elected as its president. Despite death threats, bombings of Black leaders' homes, and arrests, the boycott ended in victory when the U.S. Supreme Court ruled in 1956 that segregated seating on public buses was unconstitutional.

This protest launched the modern Civil Rights Movement, but it was met with escalating violence. Churches were bombed, Black-owned businesses destroyed, and leaders were routinely harassed or killed. One of the most horrific attacks came on September 15, 1963, when white supremacists bombed the 16th Street Baptist Church in Birmingham, Alabama, killing four little girls—Addie Mae Collins, Cynthia Wesley, Carole Robertson, and Denise McNair. It shocked the world and galvanized the movement.

Earlier that year, Reverend George Lee and Lamar Smith were murdered for registering Black voters in Mississippi. And just two months later, the nation would be horrified by the lynching of 14-year-old Emmett Till, whose brutal death would help awaken a global movement for justice.

In Birmingham, Police Commissioner Bull Connor, a symbol of white supremacist authority, unleashed police dogs and fire hoses on peaceful protesters, including children. Connor worked hand-in-hand with the Klan to silence the movement through terror. But the world was watching. President John F. Kennedy was forced to respond and condemned segregation publicly, acknowledging the courage of those demanding change.

Throughout the 1950s and '60s, Black protesters faced violence, arrests, and state-sanctioned oppression. Yet their demand for justice never wavered. They fought for the right to vote, to live without fear, to be treated with dignity—and they paid the price in blood. The freedom they pursued was not freely given. It had to be demanded. It had to be defended. And it continues to be fought for today.

The Murder of Emmett Till and the Spark of a Movement

On August 28, 1955, 14-year-old Emmett Till was lynched in Money, Mississippi, for reportedly saying "Bye, baby" to Carolyn Bryant, a 21-year-old white woman and the wife of a local grocery store owner. Emmett was abducted from his great-uncle's home in the middle of the night by Roy Bryant and his half-brother, J.W. Milam—two white men who acted with impunity in a region ruled by white terror.

Three days later, Emmett's body was pulled from the Tallahatchie River, tied to a 70-pound cotton gin fan with barbed wire wrapped around his neck. He had been tortured—shot in the head, his eye gouged out, his skull crushed. The brutality of the crime was meant to send a message to all Black people who dared to challenge white supremacy.

His mother, Mamie Till-Mobley, demanded an open-casket funeral in Chicago, forcing America and the world to face the horror of what racism truly looked like. The image of Emmett's mutilated body was a turning point in the Civil Rights Movement.

Despite testimony from Emmett's uncle, Moses Wright, who bravely pointed out the killers in court, an all-white jury acquitted Roy Bryant and J.W. Milam. Protected by double jeopardy laws, the two later confessed to the murder in a paid magazine interview, boasting about their crime. Justice was not even an option in a system that was built to protect whiteness.

Medgar Evers, a WWII veteran and NAACP field secretary, became one of the most prominent civil rights leaders in Mississippi. After returning from Europe, he applied to the

University of Mississippi Law School, only to be rejected because he was Black—a reminder that in Jim Crow America, even veterans who served their country were denied fundamental rights.

On June 11, 1963, Evers was assassinated in his driveway, in front of his children, by white supremacist Byron De La Beckwith. It would take over 30 years for Beckwith to be convicted—proof that Black lives were treated as disposable by both the courts and the culture.

Just a year later, during Freedom Summer of 1964, three young civil rights workers—James Chaney, a Black Mississippian, and two white allies, Andrew Goodman and Michael Schwerner—were kidnapped, murdered, and buried in an earthen dam by the Ku Klux Klan, with help from local law enforcement. They had been arrested under false charges, released to a waiting mob, and disappeared into the dark backroads of Mississippi.

The murder of Goodman, Chaney, and Schwerner exposed the unholy alliance between white supremacy and the state. Nearly 40 Black churches were burned that summer alone. While civil rights leaders organized for voting rights and education, the FBI was busy wiretapping and surveilling Dr. Martin Luther King Jr., treating him as a national threat instead of a national hero.

The Caste System and Divide in Rwanda and Burundi

While African Americans were fighting against Jim Crow and racial segregation in the West, many African nations were grappling with a different form of white supremacy: the imported Aryan caste system. European colonial powers intentionally used race, class, and physical features to divide Indigenous African communities that had once lived together in peace.

One of the clearest examples of this colonial manipulation occurred in Rwanda and Burundi. The Tutsi, who were generally lighter-skinned and taller, were favored by Belgian and French colonizers, while the Hutu majority, darker and more rural, were treated as inferior. Europeans racialized these differences, creating an artificial caste system that turned neighbors into enemies.

Colonial powers introduced ethnic ID cards, legally distinguishing Tutsis from Hutus and enforcing a social hierarchy rooted in appearance and privilege, not in cultural difference. The truth is, the Hutus and Tutsis spoke the same language, shared religious beliefs, and had a long history of intermarriage. But colonizers used their caste playbook, just as had been done in India and later in Jim Crow America, to destroy that unity.

Though Germany was late to the scramble for Africa, it too adopted this racial strategy when it colonized Rwanda and Burundi before World War I. After Germany's defeat, Belgium inherited control, continuing to privilege the Tutsi minority, placing them in schools, political offices, and elite circles while excluding the Hutus.

When Belgium shifted its support in 1959, it allowed the Hutu majority to participate in elections and dismantled the Tutsi monarchy. Rwanda was granted independence in 1962 with Hutus in power, while Burundi remained Tutsi-led. What followed was not peace, but decades of ethnic violence, all seeded by Europe's racist and manipulative colonial policies.

By the 1990s, a new wave of conflict erupted. Tutsi refugees from Uganda and Burundi launched a military campaign to challenge the Hutu-led government in Rwanda. The result was one of the most horrific genocides in modern history. After a plane carrying the presidents of Rwanda and Burundi was shot down on April 6, 1994, the genocide began.

In just 100 days, over 800,000 Tutsis and moderate Hutus were murdered. Militias targeted children, pregnant women, and entire families. The international community stood by in silence while the United Nations prioritized evacuating white Europeans and Americans, leaving the Black Tutsi population to die.

By the time Paul Kagame led a successful military resistance and signed a peace treaty in 1995, millions were dead or displaced. The caste system, imported by white colonizers, had turned cultural siblings into deadly rivals.

This tragedy is not just about Rwanda or Burundi—it is a blueprint of colonialism's impact. Whether in India, Africa, or the Americas, the caste system of whiteness has always functioned to divide Black and brown communities, enforce economic dependency, and uphold white supremacy.

During the same era that Jim Crow laws gripped Black communities in the United States, South Africa was locked in a brutal caste system known as apartheid—a legalized structure of white domination that oppressed Black Africans through land theft, forced relocation, and racial segregation.

South Africa had been colonized by the Dutch and British as early as the 17th century. However, apartheid was formally institutionalized after the 1948 election, when the National Party came to power and reestablished racial separation to uphold white supremacy. Interracial marriage was banned, and Black South Africans were forcibly removed from cities and relocated to distant "tribal homelands" in rural areas to isolate them from economic centers.

Black workers were separated from their families, forced into low-paying, dangerous labor on white-owned farms and mines, while their land was confiscated. Those who resisted saw their crops burned, their communities starved, and their people imprisoned or killed.

In 1950, the Population Registration Act classified every citizen into a racial group: white, Indian, colored, or Black, with Black people ranked at the bottom. The 1951 Prevention of Illegal Squatting Act allowed forced evictions, while the Abolition of Passes Act forced all Black people to carry passbooks listing their race, job, and address. Without this document, they could be arrested just for entering white areas. These laws echoed the slave pass laws of 1760, reinforcing the belief that Black lives were property to be controlled.

Despite these brutal policies, resistance grew. On March 21, 1960, a peaceful anti-pass protest in the township of Sharpeville turned into a massacre when South African police opened fire on the crowd, killing 69 people and wounding over 200. The rally was organized by the Pan Africanist Congress (PAC), led by Robert Sobukwe, who was arrested and later imprisoned.

In the aftermath, the South African government banned the African National Congress (ANC) and PAC, and cracked down using the Ninety-Day Act, which allowed arrests without trial. But resistance intensified. The ANC formed Umkhonto we Sizwe (Spear of the Nation), and the PAC formed Poqo, both armed wings to fight apartheid through sabotage and guerrilla tactics, trained in Ghana, Tanzania, and Zambia.

Nelson Mandela, who led Umkhonto, was arrested in 1962—allegedly with help from the CIA—and sentenced to life in prison along with other ANC leaders at the Rivonia Treason Trial. Despite the government's repression, international pressure grew. Athletes, artists, and businesses boycotted South Africa, while protests erupted around the world against apartheid's cruelty.

On June 16, 1976, thousands of Black students in Soweto protested the government's racist education policies. The peaceful march turned deadly when police opened fire, killing as many as 700 students. The uprising sparked a national revolt led by youth, and the Black Consciousness Movement, headed by Steve Biko, gained momentum.

Biko was arrested in 1977, tortured, and murdered in police custody. But his message lived on. His death revealed the extreme brutality of the apartheid regime to the world and inspired a new wave of resistance.

By the late 1980s, the apartheid regime was unraveling under the weight of international sanctions, internal resistance, and global condemnation. In 1990, President F.W. de Klerk lifted the ban on the ANC and released Nelson Mandela after 27 years in prison.

In April 1994, South Africa held its first democratic elections. Mandela was elected the first Black president, and the ANC became the ruling party, ending 46 years of official apartheid and centuries of colonial domination.

"For a mere moment I have forsaken you, but with great mercies
I will gather you... No weapon formed against you shall prosper,
and you shall condemn every tongue which rises against you in
judgment."

(Isaiah 54:7–17)

South Africa's liberation was not just political—it was spiritual. It reflected the ongoing struggle of Black people worldwide who continue to resist systems of caste, domination, and racial hierarchy. Just as the Aryan caste system was used to divide Africans in Rwanda and India, apartheid in South Africa was another front in the global war against Black liberation.

The rise of Mandela, the youth uprisings, and the defiant spirit of Steve Biko were not isolated events. They were part of a divine movement to restore dignity to the oppressed and bring down the spiritual strongholds of white supremacy.

CHAPTER 13

God's Judgment

The Book of Ezekiel opens with the prophet living in exile, a captive near the Chebar River, southeast of Babylon. In 597 BCE, Ezekiel, just 25 years old, was taken from Jerusalem during the second Babylonian invasion under Nebuchadnezzar, along with thousands of Judah's upper class. Five years into exile, Ezekiel received a vision from God, a calling to prophetic ministry amid oppression and rebellion.

"The heavens were opened, and I saw visions of God."

(Ezekiel 1:1)

In a vision rich with symbols, Ezekiel described a radiant cloud of fire emerging from the north, with four living creatures—

each bearing the face of a man, a lion, an ox, and an eagle. Above them stood a crystal firmament, and above that, a throne of sapphire surrounded by fire and brightness. Ezekiel fell to his face as the Spirit of the Lord lifted him and gave him his assignment:

"Son of man, I am sending you to a rebellious nation…they are stubborn children. Whether they listen or not, they will know that a prophet has been among them."

(Ezekiel 2:35)

Ezekiel was sent to call out Israel's sins, but his message extended beyond Jerusalem. He pronounced judgment on neighboring nations like Ammon, Moab, Tyre, Sidon, Edom, Egypt, and Ethiopia. These nations had broken the covenant, turned to idolatry, and rejected their identity as the firstborn people of God. They were warned of destruction for adopting foreign religions and abandoning divine law.

"You feared the sword; I will bring the sword upon you…because you went as a harlot after the Gentiles, defiled by their idols."

(Ezekiel 23–24)

Ezekiel's prophecy revealed a transfer of power from the Hebrew people to Gentile empires that did not know the Creator. He warned of an era ruled by empires fueled by idolatry, military conquest, and caste oppression—from Babylon to Rome to today's Eurocentric powers.

"It will be a day of clouds, the Time of the Gentiles...Ethiopia, Libya, Lydia...shall fall by the sword."

(Ezekiel 30:4 6)

Jesus later confirmed this prophecy:

"Jerusalem will be trampled by Gentiles until the times of the Gentiles are fulfilled. Then they will see the Son of Man coming with power and great glory."

(Luke 21:24 27)

In one of his most famous visions, Ezekiel is led to a valley of dry bones—a symbol of a scattered, lifeless nation. The bones are reassembled, covered in flesh, but still lifeless—until the breath of God brings them back to life. This is a vision of restoration, not just for ancient Israel but for every oppressed people scattered by slavery and colonization.

*"Behold, O My people, I will open your graves...
and bring you into the land of Israel."*

(Ezekiel 37)

This resurrection pointed to a future awakening—not only of national identity but of spiritual truth and justice. It was a promise for a people written off as dead to rise again with purpose and dignity.

Prophetic Judgment and Hope

After the fall of Jerusalem, many Hebrews fled to Upper Egypt, settling in a region known as Pathros, now part of northern Sudan—a region still suffering from poverty and civil war. In modern times, colorism and caste oppression have divided Sudan, with lighter-skinned Arabs in the north and darker-skinned Africans in the south, fueling decades of violence.

This division—like in India, South Africa, or Rwanda—was engineered through colonialism, separating people by race, shade, and class. The Euro-caste system, rooted in white supremacy and Aryan ideology, has hidden its evil hands across the four corners of the world.

The prophet Zephaniah echoed Ezekiel's message. Though he began with judgment—against both Israel and Ethiopia—he ended with a promise of restoration:

"From beyond the rivers of Ethiopia, My worshippers...shall bring My offering. I will restore to the peoples a pure language, that they may call upon the name of the Lord...At that time, I will bring you back... and give you fame and praise among all the peoples of the earth."

(Zephaniah 3:9–19)

Despite conquest, colonialism, slavery, and systemic erasure, a remnant remains—rooted in covenant, truth, and divine justice. The time of the Gentiles may have flourished through conquest and exploitation, but it will not last forever.

In the year King Uzziah of Judah died, the prophet Isaiah received his first vision from the Lord. He saw God seated on a majestic throne, and the train of His robe filled the temple.

Above the throne stood fiery seraphim with six wings, and their voices shook the very foundations of the doors while smoke filled the air.

Isaiah, overwhelmed by the holiness of God and his own unworthiness, cried out:

"Woe is me, for I am undone! Because I am a man of unclean lips, and I live among a people of unclean lips. For my eyes have seen the King, the Lord of Hosts."

(Isaiah 6:5)

One of the seraphim touched Isaiah's lips with a burning coal from the altar, symbolizing his cleansing and commission. But Isaiah's prophetic assignment would be a hard one: he was to deliver a message of judgment and warning to a rebellious people who had turned away from God.

The Lord declared that the people would not listen, and their spiritual blindness would bring devastation—not just to Israel and Judah, but to the entire Kushite region as well. Idolatry, materialism, and trust in Gentile alliances had corrupted the land, especially along the Mediterranean and into Africa. Though the prophets warned them, the people chose the seductive comfort of foreign powers over faithfulness to their covenant.

Habakkuk and Babylon's Judgment

During the Babylonian advance, the prophet Habakkuk was overwhelmed by the violence and injustice he witnessed. He questioned God directly:

*"Why do You tolerate the treacherous? Why are the wicked
devouring people more righteous than they?"*

(Habakkuk 1:13)

Reports came in that the Kushites along the Nile—once
trusted allies of Israel—were under attack and paying heavy
tribute to Babylon:

*"I saw the tents of Cushan in affliction;
the curtains of the land of Midian trembled."*

(Habakkuk 3:7)

Babylon, a brutal empire, was sweeping through the region
with terrifying force. Backed by loose alliances of Assyrian,
Chaldean, and Scythian warriors, their rise mirrored later
European colonial tactics—imperial violence in the name of
economic conquest. Their deep roots in ancient Balkan tribes
foreshadowed a violent legacy of white supremacy, caste, and
empire that continues to this day.

God revealed to Habakkuk that He was using Babylon as
an instrument of judgment against the covenant people who
had betrayed divine justice:

*"I am raising up the Chaldeans, a bitter and hasty nation... they
take what is not theirs. Their horses are swifter than leopards... they
gather captives like sand. They worship their own power as god."*

(Habakkuk 1:6–11)

Rather than pleading for Babylon's defeat, Habakkuk grieved
over the moral failure of his own people. He asked why violence

and injustice were allowed to grow unchecked, even among those who should have known better.

God commanded Isaiah to walk naked and barefoot for three years, symbolizing the coming shame and defeat of Egypt and Ethiopia. It was a striking message to Judah, who had placed its faith in African military alliances rather than the God of Justice:

"I will also make you a light to the Gentiles, that you may bring My salvation to the ends of the earth."

(Isaiah 49:6)

Isaiah asked how long the people must suffer. God answered:

"Until the cities lie in ruins and no one is left."

(Isaiah 6:11)

Judah trusted Kushite's military strength, but Isaiah warned: no nation, system, or empire can save us when we've abandoned righteousness. The same message echoes today in a world obsessed with alliances, nationalism, and militarized power structures—still blind to the call of true justice.

CHAPTER 14

Restoration of the Hebrew People

T he prophet Isaiah received a vision not just of Israel's judgment—but of the eventual downfall of the Gentile empires who had enslaved and oppressed God's people. In Isaiah 47, the prophet speaks directly to Babylon, the symbol of global domination and white imperial power:

"Come down and sit in the dust, O virgin daughter of Babylon; sit on the ground without a throne, O daughter of the Chaldeans!"

(Isaiah 47:1)

God had allowed Babylon to rise, but it showed no mercy. Its arrogance and violence against the covenant people would not go unpunished:

"I was angry with My people; I gave them into your hands.
But you showed them no mercy—even the elderly were crushed
under your yoke."

(Isaiah 47:6)

This prophecy parallels the final judgment in the Book of Revelation, where John sees the seals opened and the Gentile powers judged by plagues: floods, famine, fire, and war. The same kingdoms that rose through conquest, colonization, and exploitation will be brought low.

Despite the suffering, Isaiah also delivers a message of hope: God has not forgotten His people, the Israelites and Africans. A time of healing, justice, and return is promised:

"In the day of salvation, I will help you. I will preserve you and
make you a covenant to the people, to restore the earth..."

(Isaiah 49:8)

God promises that those who once oppressed and consumed the people would be brought low, and that the nations would finally recognize the divine favor upon the Afro-Semitic people:

"I will feed those who oppress you with their own flesh...
All flesh shall know that I, the Lord, am your Savior and Redeemer,
the Mighty One of Jacob."

(Isaiah 49:26)

In Isaiah 60, we are given a vision of global restoration—of people of African descent rising from centuries of oppression and returning to power:

> *"Arise, shine, for your light has come! The glory of the Lord is risen upon you... The wealth of the Gentiles shall come to you."*
>
> (Isaiah 60:1-5)

The Sahara and Aswan will no longer be wastelands. Africa will flourish again. Those who once exploited African lands and peoples will return in submission:

> *"The sons of those who afflicted you will come bowing... all who despised you shall fall at your feet."*
>
> (Isaiah 60:14)

This prophecy speaks not only of spiritual salvation but also of economic justice, cultural restoration, and divine vindication for the scattered children of the diaspora.

The Messianic Servant and the Dawn of Justice

In the Book of Revelation, John—exiled on Patmos for speaking the truth—receives visions of the collapse of Mystery Babylon, a symbol of global imperialism, white supremacy, and false religion:

> *"Babylon the great is fallen... She has become a dwelling place for demons... for all nations have drunk of the wine of her immorality."*
>
> (Revelation 18:2-3)

Just as Isaiah declared, "Arise, shine," John hears a voice from heaven calling the oppressed to separate from the system that enslaved them:

"Come out of her, My people, lest you share in her sins... for her sins have reached to heaven, and God has remembered her iniquities."

(Revelation 18:4-5)

This judgment is not abstract—it is specific and historical: The same global systems that profited off genocide, slavery, caste, and colonization will be held accountable.

"In the same measure she glorified herself and lived in luxury, give her torment and sorrow."

(Revelation 18:7)

The True Justice of the Servant of the Lord

Isaiah's vision ends not with vengeance, but with the emergence of the Messianic Servant, the one who will bring true justice, not through conquest, but through truth and righteousness:

"Behold! My Servant, whom I uphold... I have put My Spirit upon Him. He will bring forth justice to the Gentiles... He will not grow weary till He has established justice on the earth."

(Isaiah 42:1 4)

This message speaks clearly to our moment in history, when the systems of empire, racism, and caste are beginning to collapse. The time is coming when the first will be last, and the last will be first. It is a warning to the oppressor and a promise to the oppressed: God sees, remembers, and will restore.

The Illusion of Equality and the Persistence of Caste

The illusion of racial equality in America was never meant to be real. While Black people fought for freedom and civil rights, white society-built wealth and equity with full support from the government. True Black independence was earned through generations of blood, sweat, and suffering—but never truly guaranteed.

Every effort to break free from the caste system has been met with violence, deceit, or delay. The struggle against injustice continues to this day. America's obsession with power, greed, and division has rotted its moral foundation, and history's pain has been buried beneath empty promises and whitewashed narratives.

The caste system in the U.S.—much like the Hindu caste system in India—was engineered to uphold white dominance and suppress Black and brown communities. Policies like redlining, underfunded schools, and unequal access to housing and capital have kept Black neighborhoods locked in generational poverty. Meanwhile, affirmative action, meant to level the playing field, is criticized even though white women are its greatest beneficiaries.

Black Americans have long been denied fairness in the courts, education, and the economy. Protests against police brutality are not new, but social media has helped bring long-ignored violence into the spotlight. The murder of George

Floyd in 2020 by Minneapolis police officer Derek Chauvin reignited global protests. Floyd's killing followed the deaths of Ahmaud Arbery, Breonna Taylor, and many others whose lives were taken without justice.

In Kenosha, Wisconsin, after police shot Jacob Blake seven times in the back, protesters were met with violence. Seventeen-year-old Kyle Rittenhouse traveled across state lines, shot three people, and walked away untouched by police. In contrast, Dijon Kizzee was killed in Los Angeles for a bicycle violation, Atatiana Jefferson was shot through her bedroom window in Texas, and Amir Locke was killed during a no-knock raid in Minneapolis. All were Black. None were given a chance to explain.

In Memphis, five Black police officers brutally beat 29-year-old Tyre Nichols to death—exposing how deeply white supremacy has infiltrated systems of power, even though those who share the same skin color as their victims. This was not just police violence—it was a reflection of how the culture of policing in America often upholds racialized brutality, regardless of the officer's race.

At Nichols' funeral, Vice President Kamala Harris spoke to the nation's conscience, stating, "If it is not in the interest of public safety, then Tyre Nichols should be here today."

Yet justice remains elusive. On May 7, 2025, three of the former Memphis officers were found not guilty of state charges. Two others had previously pleaded guilty to federal civil rights violations, acknowledging the brutality. But the outcome underscores a troubling pattern: accountability in cases of police violence—especially against Black bodies—is still the exception, not the rule.

Tyre Nichols' death is not an isolated tragedy. It is part of a much larger system that devalues Black life and recycles violence through institutions built on control, not care. His story reminds us that true reform cannot come without dismantling the deeper structures that enable and protect state-sanctioned violence—even when it's carried out by those who look like us.

White Supremacy Is a System—Not Just a Belief

Racism in America isn't just about individual hatred—it's a system embedded in policing, the courts, politics, and even religious institutions. White supremacy has shaped these systems to privilege whiteness while keeping Black and Brown communities locked into second-class status. It doesn't just operate through violence—it thrives through laws, traditions, and narratives that celebrate whiteness as the norm and treat everyone else as "other."

During a time when the nation was forced to confront racial injustice, President Donald Trump inflamed the crisis. In his first term, he called racial justice protestors "thugs" and defended Confederate symbols. He mocked Bubba Wallace—NASCAR's only full-time Black driver—after a noose was discovered in his garage. Trump's rhetoric gave cover to white nationalist groups, embracing language that echoed the propaganda of Nazi Germany: portraying minorities as threats and idolizing a past rooted in racial dominance.

His mishandling of the COVID-19 pandemic only magnified the injustice. By calling it the "China Virus," denying its severity, and pushing herd immunity, Trump showed a dangerous disregard for the lives of the poor, the elderly, and communities of color. These were the very people most affected—those with the least access to healthcare and support. Once again, America's racial hierarchy meant the difference between life and death.

In his second term, President Donald Trump doubled down on policies that amplified America's racial caste system. From pardoning war criminals to defending Confederate monuments, Trump glorified white nationalist symbols while attacking civil rights gains. His administration openly targeted Diversity, Equity, and Inclusion (DEI) efforts, rolled back affirmative action to pre-1965 standards, and encouraged a climate of fear by labeling civil servants as "DEI snitches."

Trump's hardline immigration agenda also exposed the cruelty embedded in U.S. policy. One deeply unpopular proposal involved deporting undocumented immigrants to prisons in El Salvador—an idea 61% of Americans rejected. He also moved to suspend asylum applications and pushed for increased workplace raids by ICE. Public opinion remained divided, but more Americans opposed these measures than supported them.

Trump's policies did not emerge in a vacuum. They followed a long legacy of racialized governance. Ronald Reagan, often idolized by the political right, also fueled racial inequality through his War on Drugs—disproportionately targeting Black and Brown communities—and by backing authoritarian regimes in Central America. These actions helped destabilize the region and contributed directly to the immigration crises we face today.

The through line from Reagan to Trump is clear: a politics of fear, exclusion, and control—designed to uphold white dominance under the guise of law and order. But history demands accountability. Until these systems are dismantled, the violence they produce—whether at the border, in prisons, or in police encounters—will continue to shape the lives of the most vulnerable.

Reagan's administration allowed crack cocaine to flood Black communities while blocking efforts to end apartheid in South Africa. Congress eventually overrode his veto to pass the Civil Rights Restoration Act and impose sanctions on South Africa. However, the damage to Black neighborhoods in the U.S. was already done.

Trump and Reagan both catered to white grievance and economic elitism. Their rhetoric and policies encouraged the spread of systemic racism under the guise of patriotism and moral order. From Reagan's "War on Drugs" to Trump's "Make America Great Again," both slogans signaled a return to a time when white dominance was unquestioned—and that is exactly what their supporters craved.

The same playbook that once glorified the Confederacy and fueled segregation now hides behind modern conservatism. The goal remains the same: to keep Black and brown people powerless, voiceless, and economically dependent. The caste system has not disappeared—it has simply evolved, hidden in plain sight.

White Supremacy on Trial: From Trump to the Capitol Insurrection

During the first presidential debate against Joe Biden, President Donald Trump was asked to condemn white supremacist groups. Instead of disavowing them, he told the Proud Boys to "stand back and stand by," while blaming "antifa and the left." In that moment, Trump confirmed what many already knew—he wasn't just tolerating white supremacy; he was weaponizing it.

Throughout his presidency, Trump fed America's deep-rooted caste system. He created chaos to divide, used racism to distract, and praised symbols of oppression. He called racial justice protesters "thugs," defended the Confederate flag, and mocked Bubba Wallace after a noose was found in his garage. Trump turned the presidency into a stage where white nationalism could perform unchecked.

America's foundation—like a house built on sand—was always unstable because it was built on stolen land and white supremacy. Systemic racism remains the storm that threatens to wash it all away. Even during a deadly pandemic, more people voted for Trump in 2020 than in 2016. That support wasn't just about politics—it was about preserving a centuries-old caste system rooted in racial dominance.

As his defeat neared, Trump's allies spread lies about election fraud. His lawyer Rudy Giuliani fanned conspiracy theories, and far-right media flooded the internet with propaganda. Then came January 6, 2021.

At a rally near the Capitol, Trump told his supporters, "You will never take back our country with weakness. Fight like hell." His son, Donald Jr., added, "We are coming for you," targeting lawmakers who refused to overturn the election.

The mob stormed the U.S. Capitol, waving Confederate flags and wearing antisemitic slogans. They smashed windows, vandalized offices, and chanted "Hang Mike Pence" while hunting Speaker Nancy Pelosi. A gallow was erected on the Capitol lawn. This wasn't just a riot—it was a resurrection of the Confederacy in the halls of Capitol Hill.

Despite the violence, many rioters received lenient treatment: bail, house arrest, or release to family. Some Capitol police were charged with helping them. Meanwhile, Black protesters demanding justice have long been met with tear gas, rubber bullets, and mass arrests. The contrast was undeniable—and deeply racial.

Trump later praised the insurrectionists as "very special people" and promised pardons if reelected. Former Attorney General William Barr called the event a "betrayal of [Trump's] office," but 21 Republican lawmakers still voted against honoring officers who defended the Capitol.

On the first day of his second term, President Donald Trump issued over 1,500 pardons and commutations to individuals charged or convicted for their roles in the January 6th Capitol insurrection. Instead of condemning the attack on democracy, Trump embraced the rioters—calling them "patriots" and positioning them as political victims.

Even more disturbing, Trump floated the idea of offering financial compensation or reparations to those prosecuted for the violent uprising. While peaceful Black protesters have long faced criminalization and state violence for demanding justice, Trump's actions rewarded white extremists who attempted to overthrow the government.

This move sent a clear message: in Trump's America, white violence is not only excused—it is honored and potentially paid for. It was not just a political stunt; it was a declaration that the machinery of power still serves white supremacy, not democracy.

One of those officers, Michael Fanone, was beaten unconscious and tasered while screaming, "I have kids!" Still, some lawmakers downplayed the attack—calling the rioters "tourists." Trump labeled them "patriots."

The truth was clear: while Colin Kaepernick was vilified for kneeling in peaceful protest, white extremists who attacked democracy were honored by the former president. January 6 showed that white supremacy is not just alive—it is protected and celebrated by powerful figures in American politics.

Trump's rise wasn't a break from history—it was a continuation. Like Ronald Reagan before him, Trump catered to white fear and targeted communities of color. Reagan's war on drugs devastated Black neighborhoods. His foreign policies destabilized Central America and ignored apartheid in South Africa until the government was forced to act.

Trump brought these same strategies back—denying COVID-19's severity, calling it the "China Virus," and embracing herd immunity, even as the virus ravaged poor and Black communities. His slogan, "Make America Great Again," echoed Confederate nostalgia and Nazi-era ideas of racial purity.

His abuses didn't stop at home. He pressured Ukraine to investigate Biden, praised Putin's invasion of Ukraine, and was impeached twice—choosing personal power over democratic principles.

Even after the insurrection, Trump stood by the mob. Meanwhile, those who dared to speak out—like Officer Fanone and pro-democracy lawmakers—were threatened or ignored. Trump's base stayed loyal, proving that for many, white supremacy was more important than democracy itself.

Confederate flags inside the Capitol. Racist double standards in policing. Black lawmakers expelled for protesting gun violence, while their white colleague remained. This isn't just inequality—it's casteism in real time.

The greatest threat to American democracy is not those who resist injustice—it is the system of white supremacy that punishes them for doing so.

The New Face of Caste

Under Donald Trump's second administration, alongside the influence of J.D. and Elon Musk, America witnessed a deepening pattern of authoritarian retaliation and systemic attacks on racial equity. The administration aggressively targeted Diversity, Equity, and Inclusion (DEI) programs, portraying them as divisive rather than acknowledging them as long-overdue efforts to address centuries of institutional racism. A glaring example was the unprecedented removal of the Black Joint Chiefs Chair—widely seen as retaliation for his perceived support of DEI principles.

With the help of right-wing voices like Pete Hegseth, Trump turned DEI into a political scapegoat, using it to rally his base while gutting programs intended to uplift marginalized communities. What he called "eliminating division" was really about protecting whiteness and erasing any progress toward racial accountability.

Trump also pushed for sweeping purges within federal institutions, promising to fire public servants who challenged his worldview or refused to enforce racially regressive policies. He proposed defunding Historically Black Colleges and Universities (HBCUs) and slashing critical support for health care, nutrition, and disability assistance—policies that disproportionately harm Black, Brown, and Indigenous families. These were not just budget cuts—they were deliberate efforts to deepen suffering among the most vulnerable, all while redirecting wealth to the ultra-rich through corporate tax breaks.

The Trump administration's 2025 agenda—spearheaded through initiatives like Project 2025—marks a radical rollback of federal support for diversity, equity, and inclusion (DEI) efforts and programs that serve historically marginalized communities.

Executive Order 14151, signed on January 20, 2025, is at the heart of this shift and is titled "Ending Radical and Wasteful Government DEI Programs and Preferencing." This order eliminates all DEI-related mandates, policies, and positions across federal agencies. It also directs agencies to report all DEI and "environmental justice" employees to the Office of Management and Budget within 60 days—a move critics liken to political targeting and intimidation.

Environmental Justice Betrayed

In a deeply troubling move, the U.S. Department of Justice (DOJ) under President Donald Trump's second administration terminated a landmark environmental justice settlement meant to address the long-standing sewage crisis in Lowndes County, Alabama—a historically Black, rural community plagued for generations by failing sanitation systems and government neglect.

Citing Trump's Executive Order banning Diversity, Equity, and Inclusion (DEI) initiatives, the DOJ framed environmental justice efforts as "distortions of the national interest." Assistant Attorney General Harmeet K. Dhillon bluntly stated that the DOJ would no longer "waste" taxpayer dollars on what she dismissed as "environmental justice through a DEI lens"—a chilling reminder that, in the eyes of America's ruling elites, Black suffering remains expendable.

Under President Biden, the DOJ had secured a 2023 settlement with the Alabama Department of Public Health (ADPH) after an investigation exposed systemic neglect, forcing residents to live with raw sewage in their homes and communities. That agreement required ADPH to suspend penalties against families with inadequate septic systems and to draft a long-term plan to repair the region's crumbling sanitation infrastructure.

Trump's return to power reversed all progress. The DOJ's withdrawal not only abandoned the federal commitment to repair environmental injustices but also sent a broader political message: racial inequality, especially in public health, would no longer be officially acknowledged, let alone addressed.

Though the ADPH claims it will continue limited efforts to install septic systems, it openly admits that true, lasting solutions fall outside its authority. Without federal enforcement, Lowndes County remains trapped in a cycle of poverty, disease infested, and political abandonment.

This is not an isolated incident—it is a national warning. It reveals what happens when the government retreats from accountability and treats Black life as disposable in the name of political expediency.

The rollback in Lowndes County is part of a wider strategy: to erase systemic racism from public discourse, dismantle protections for vulnerable communities, and fortify a caste system that privileges the powerful while leaving the oppressed to fend for themselves.

Lowndes County is a powerful symbol of America's unfinished reckoning with its caste-driven foundations. When government agencies side with pollution over people, they clarify that justice is not guaranteed for all, and for some, survival remains negotiable.

The administration's proposals in education strike at the foundation of equity. Project 2025 recommends eliminating Title I of the Elementary and Secondary Education Act of 1965, effectively gutting $18 billion in federal funds that support schools in low-income communities. It also seeks to abolish Head Start, a program that has supported the early development of children from underserved families for decades.

These actions have not gone unchallenged. The NAACP filed a lawsuit against the U.S. Department of Education, alleging that defunding schools with DEI programs amounts to unlawfully discriminating against Black students and undermining their constitutional right to equal educational opportunity.

The Battle Over Higher Education: Harvard vs. Trump.

In one of the most visible clashes, Harvard University has openly defied Trump's demands to dismantle its DEI initiatives and overhaul its hiring and admissions practices. The administration retaliated by freezing $2.3 billion in federal grants and contracts and threatening to withhold up to $9 billion. It even pressured the IRS to revoke Harvard's tax-exempt status—a clear act of political reprisal.

Harvard President Alan Garber declared that the university would not "surrender its independence or relinquish its constitutional rights," defending academic freedom and institutional autonomy in the face of federal overreach. This standoff reflects a deeper national conflict over who controls truth, education, and public discourse.

Economic Nationalism or Economic Punishment?

Trump's domestic policies are matched by an aggressive international agenda. His proposed tariff expansions, affecting trade with up to 185 countries, risk destabilizing global markets and driving up prices for American consumers. These moves are not about economic fairness—they are about punishing political dissent, isolating allies, and reinforcing a caste-based system that protects the wealth and power of the elite while ignoring the suffering of working-class families and communities of color.

Colorism, Colonialism, and Systemic Oppression

Behind the language of "merit-based systems" and "efficiency," Trump's 2025 plan signals a re-entrenchment of racial hierarchy and economic segregation—an attempt to restore the same caste logic that has historically excluded Black, Brown, and Indigenous people from equal opportunity. In this new form of governance, loyalty is rewarded, equity is vilified, and justice is optional.

This is not just policy—it is a modern form of systemic re-colonization, cloaked in nationalism but rooted in oppression.

Racism in America is like a tsunami. It may seem calm on the surface, but deep beneath the waves, it builds with force, ready to sweep away truth, justice, and progress. From colonialism to colorism, from slavery to segregation, the caste system continues to haunt the present.

In Africa, we see this legacy too. Decades after colonialism, skin bleaching remains popular, fueled by media, beauty standards, and internalized racism. The darker your skin, the more you are told to change it, despite Africa being the cradle of civilization.

Colorism, born of colonialism and caste, has left lasting scars. From actresses pressured to lighten their skin to mothers bleaching their children, the message is clear: whiteness is still seen as superior.

However, that must change.

We must speak the truth, remember history, and resist the systems—seen and unseen—that seek to divide and destroy us.

Caste, Color, and the Global Logic of White Supremacy

In the American South, Jim Crow laws enforced racial apartheid—legalized oppression that echoed the violence of slavery. Segregation wasn't just about keeping Black people apart from white society; it was about keeping them beneath it. Denied access to quality housing, education, public services, and fair employment, Black communities were locked out of opportunity and stripped of dignity.

This didn't happen by accident. America's caste system was designed to protect white dominance—preserving elite bloodlines at the top while keeping Black and Brown people locked at the bottom. Since the nation's founding, race and caste have determined who gets access to opportunity and who is left behind.

And this system is not exclusive to the United States. In India, a similar caste hierarchy reinforces color-based oppression. The darkest-skinned Indians—especially those from Dalit or "Untouchable" communities—have long been treated as impure, unworthy of dignity. Today, that same bias persists in Indian media. Bollywood rarely casts dark-skinned actors in lead roles, and when it does, it often darkens the skin of lighter actors instead. The 2019 film Bala was widely criticized for doing exactly that.

In the U.S., the 2015 film Skinned tackled this same obsession with skin tone. The movie follows Jolie, a young Black woman played by Jasmine Burke, who uses bleaching creams to lighten her skin. In her pursuit of beauty and acceptance, she suffers severe health consequences, including infertility—an indictment of the physical and emotional costs of colorism.

This obsession with whiteness is also a billion-dollar industry. In India, skin-lightening products are heavily promoted by celebrities who reinforce the idea that light skin equals beauty and success. Across Africa, similar products flood markets, feeding the myth that lighter skin means power, wealth, and respectability.

In African film and media, lighter-skinned actors are often favored, while darker-skinned talent is pushed aside—repeating the same colonial logic that equated whiteness with superiority and Blackness with inferiority. This is more than personal bias—it's the global legacy of white supremacy, deeply woven into how societies value skin color, beauty, and worth.

This is casteism—global, brutal, and dehumanizing.

From the slums of India to the streets of Ferguson, Black and Brown people are still fighting to be seen, heard, and treated as fully human. Across the Middle East, darker skin is often met with prejudice, exclusion, and violence. In Israel, Palestinians are routinely marginalized as "too dark" to belong, while Ethiopian Jews and other dark-skinned communities face systemic racism in housing, healthcare, and education.

Modern Echo: Gaza and the Global Color Line

The oppression of Gaza mirrors the horrors of African slavery, genocide of native Americans, and the ruthless logic of European caste colonialism. Like other colonized lands, Gaza endures a modern-day apartheid and what many now call state-sponsored genocide—where race, religion, and ethnicity determine who gets to live and who is left to die.

> "People in Gaza are neither dead nor alive, they are walking corpses." — UNRWA Aid Groups

The people of Gaza—darker-complexion with tan skinned, dispossessed, and targeted—are seen as expendable by a global caste system that views them as too dark, too poor, too Palestinian to matter. Their suffering is not isolated. It is part of a much larger global struggle against systems that demand submission and punish those who choose truth, dignity, and resistance over silence and compromise.

Today, Gaza has become a symbol of ongoing colonial violence, racial injustice, and spiritual resistance. Much like other oppressed peoples throughout history—in Africa, the Americas, and elsewhere—Palestinians are being starved or killed simply for trying to secure food, as if their lives were pieces in a cruel game.

Colorism and caste are not just cultural biases—they are embedded systems of exclusion designed to strip people of their dignity and identity. So, we must ask: How many more lives must be lost before truth becomes more than a slogan?

In corporate America, the bias is just as real. Black women are still told their natural hair is "unprofessional." Even with Ivy League degrees, they are judged for not conforming to Eurocentric beauty standards. A quick search for "unprofessional hair" brings up Black hairstyles—proof that whiteness still sets the standard for what's considered normal or acceptable.

The controversy surrounding Kyrie Irving is a case in point. He was suspended by the Brooklyn Nets after sharing a film on social media—Hebrews to Negroes: Wake Up Black America—which argues that Black people are the true descendants of the biblical Israelites. The film also contains material widely criticized as antisemitic. When Irving initially refused to apologize, the team said he was "currently unfit to be associated with the Brooklyn Nets," and Nike suspended his shoe deal. Irving later apologized and clarified his intent:

> "I stand by who I am and why I apologized. I did it because I care about my family—and I have Jewish members of my family who care for me deeply. Did the media know that? No. Everything was assumed."

He reflected:

> "I reacted instead of responding maturely. I didn't mean to be defensive. I stand by my apology, and I stand by my people."

When asked if he believed in the film's claim that Black people are the true Israelites, Irving said:

> "I was trying to better understand my heritage. Learning about the lost tribes of Israel and Black history shouldn't come at the expense of anyone else's story."

Nick Cannon faced similar backlash for saying Black people are the "true Hebrews." He praised Minister Louis Farrakhan and spoke about the erasure of Black identity in religious narratives. Cannon, who has acknowledged his own Jewish ancestry, emphasized unity, cultural pride, and the need for honest conversations about identity. His comments speak to a larger struggle—one that challenges the dominant narratives about who belongs, and who doesn't.

Even on the world stage, double standards are undeniable. Russian President Vladimir Putin recently pointed out that nearly two million Russian-speaking people live in Israel, calling it "almost a Russian-speaking country." Yet when Black people claim their ancestral ties to ancient Israel, they are mocked, erased, or branded as dangerous.

This hypocrisy is rooted in the same caste logic that has shaped America's history—where for centuries, Black Americans were forced to "stay in their place," from stepping off sidewalks to avoiding eye contact with white people. Though these acts are no longer legal, their legacy survives in modern systems that still expect Black and Brown people to submit to unspoken racial hierarchies.

If the Israelites were enslaved in Egypt during the 17th or 18th Dynasty (1600–1300 BCE), their skin tones would have reflected the Afro-Asiatic peoples of that era—ranging from deep brown to medium brown.

- The Israelites came from Canaan, part of the Afro-Asiatic cultural sphere, and ancient Canaanites were depicted with brown or copper skin (not to be confuse with the Aryan-Canaanites who were invaders of Canaan).
- Egypt at the time was ruled by African dynasties, deeply connected to Nubia, whose people were dark-skinned.
- Generations in Egypt meant cultural and genetic mixing with Egyptians and Kushites, both dark-skinned peoples.
- Biblical accounts—such as Moses marrying a Cushite

woman—reinforce this African connection.

- Ancient art shows Semitic peoples with brown skin, black hair, and features consistent with modern Ethiopians, Eritreans, Sudanese, Yemenis, and southern Palestinians—not with modern European or Arabized features.

By the time they returned to Canaan, the Israelites were a dark-skinned to medium-brown people, shaped by both their Canaanite roots and their centuries among Egyptians and Kushites.

Across history, skin color has been a foundation for caste systems. In India, the darkest-skinned—Dalits and Shudras—were forced to the bottom, excluded from full participation in society. This same logic fuels Western racism: darker skin equals less value.

At its core, white supremacy is about control—of labor, wealth, culture, and the historical narrative. It extracts resources and brilliance from Africa while denying recognition or restitution. Colonial powers rewrote history to erase African voices, glorifying European violence as "progress" and justifying exploitation as "civilization." They stole not only labor, but identity, heritage, and truth.

The Bible calls the serpent the craftiest of all creatures—and that same deceit lives on in systems that disguise theft as development, racism as order, and caste as culture. From colonial conquest to modern media, the lies persist.

But we are awake now. We are speaking. We will no longer be silent about stolen labor, erased history, or false hierarchies. The truth must be remembered, told, and defended—because liberation begins with reclaiming our story.

CHAPTER 15

The Final Reckoning of Caste and System of Empire

In the last days, Scripture says Mysterious Babylon will rise as the most powerful and wealthy nation on earth—until it faces divine judgment. The prophet Jeremiah foresaw both its meteoric rise and its sudden collapse. He warned:

> *"Though Babylon reaches the heavens and fortifies her towers,*
> *I will send plunderers against her"*

(Jeremiah 51:45-51, paraphrased).

This future empire—driven by greed, violence, and caste dominance—mirrors the systems we see today. White supremacy and casteism are not just social problems; they are spiritual diseases rooted in the original sin of pride and disobedience. These ideologies feed off domination, control, and the illusion of racial superiority.

Jeremiah prophesied about a time of trouble for the descendants of Jacob, but also a promise of liberation:

"I will break the yoke from their necks. No longer will foreigners enslave them. Instead, they will serve the Lord their God and David their king, whom I will raise for them."

(Jeremiah 30:7-8).

The empire of white supremacy, rooted in caste, slavery, and exploitation, will eventually be dismantled. All will have to reckon with their actions. Every injustice will be answered, and the freedom of God's people will be reclaimed, not through man's systems, but through divine justice.

John sees a vision of the end times in the Book of Revelation. He describes the glorified Christ with "hair like wool" and "feet like burnished bronze"—a clear symbol that the Messiah is not of European descent, but connected to the Afro-Semitic lineage often erased in modern portrayals.

John witnesses Christ open the seven seals of judgment. The Four Horsemen of the Apocalypse follow, each unleashing war, poverty, disease, and death. These horsemen are not just metaphors; they reflect the very real global consequences of imperialism, capitalism, and white supremacy. In this system:

The white horse brings conquest and cultural domination.

The red horse brings peace from the earth through war and bloodshed. The black horse represents economic injustice, where food and resources are weaponized. The pale horse symbolizes death, especially for Black, Brown, and Indigenous peoples whose lives have been deemed expendable.

As John watches, the souls of the martyrs cry out for justice, just as today's oppressed continue to protest, march, and demand to be heard.

The "mark of the beast" can be seen as the caste structure embedded in colonial capitalism—a system that ranks human worth by skin color, access to wealth, and proximity to whiteness. This caste system fuels genocide, slavery, apartheid, and the economic looting of Africa and the Americas.

More than 100 million Africans were affected by the transatlantic slave trade—over 30 million sold into slavery, and 70 million died before they reached shore.

This systemic evil, powered by greed, racism, and historical revisionism, allowed white elites to exploit African labor and resources while justifying it through religion and politics.

When Christ opens the sixth seal, the world shakes— literally and spiritually. The sun goes dark, the moon turns blood red, and the mountains fall. The entire world feels the consequences of centuries of injustice and moral decay.

Despite the suffering, humanity refuses to repent. The powerful double down on greed, violence, and exploitation. The angel declares:

> *"Babylon has fallen. Her sins have reached heaven,*
> *and God has remembered her crimes"*

(Revelation 18).

However, there is hope. The restoration of God's covenant people is also prophesied. The rejected, the enslaved, the forgotten—will rise. The tables will turn. The oppressed will inherit the earth. The children of the Diaspora, scattered across the world by force and deception, will return to their ancestral identity and be gathered by the Creator.

Isaiah saw this too:

"Arise, shine, for your light has come. The wealth of nations will come to you... and those who oppressed you will bow at your feet"

(Isaiah 60:1-14, paraphrased).

The time is coming when the lies of the caste and white supremacy will be exposed. The wealth stolen from Black and Indigenous people will be accounted for. Moreover, those who have upheld systemic injustice will face judgment, not just from history, but from the Creator.

In the end, we must choose whether to submit to the dying system of the caste or align with the kingdom of justice, equity, and truth.

For some, liberation from casteism is not even a consideration. In Scripture, Yeshua Ha'Mashiach told a rich man to sell all his possessions, give the money to the poor, and follow Him. However, the man walked away, heartbroken, because he was too attached to his wealth and status. In contrast, Abraham was wealthy but never allowed his riches to separate him from God or justify a caste system that elevated one people over another. Abraham trusted the Creator.

The global caste system is not just political—it is spiritual. It corrupts every institution: religion, economics, law, and governance. Today, more than 90% of the world's violence can be traced back to this divisive structure that ranks human beings by worth, wealth, race, and privilege.

During the Civil Rights Movement, Black Americans were hosed, beaten, lynched, and burned for daring to resist this system. The same spiritual loyalty that kept some clinging to the caste above even family or faith still dominates many hearts today. For some, the American flag and patriotism matter far less than the preservation of caste privilege. This evil yoke is embedded deep in the soul of America.

The caste elites—white supremacy at its core—has long recruited lower-class whites to help maintain the illusion of superiority. Together, they have kept Black and brown people at the bottom of every system, using race and power as the ultimate gatekeepers.

But the Bible is clear: injustice has an expiration date.

Jeremiah prophesied about the collapse of Mysterious Babylon—the wealthiest, most powerful empire of the last days. He warned that its arrogance would provoke divine judgment:

"Flee from Babylon! Save yourselves from the Lord's fierce anger... Though Babylon reaches the sky and fortifies her stronghold, I will send destroyers."

(Jeremiah 51:45-53)

This corrupt empire—young, proud, and arrogant—will fall, just as Rome fell. Caste—like Babylon, will eventually face judgment for the torment it caused. In Romans, Paul wrote:

"The wrath of God is revealed from heaven against all godlessness...
They exchanged the truth of God for a lie and worshiped created
things rather than the Creator."

(Romans 1:18-25)

In Daniel, the prophet saw a gold, silver, bronze, iron, and clay statue—symbolizing empires built on hierarchy and conquest. But a stone not cut by human hands struck and crushed the statue. The caste system, no matter how dominant, will not stand forever.

In Revelation, John describes the final world system—a political, military, economic, and spiritual empire. He calls it the beast. It looks like a lamb but speaks like a dragon. It performs signs, drops fire from the sky, and demands loyalty. Many believe this beast is a revived Roman Empire—a reborn global caste system.

Charles Darwin's "survival of the fittest" justified genocide, colonization, and the dehumanization of Indigenous and African people. The British used this ideology to exterminate Aboriginal Australians, enslave them, and strip them of their languages and identities. Colonization was not just physical— it was spiritual warfare through the caste lens.

"He causes all—small and great, rich and poor, free and slave—
to receive a mark... And no one could buy
or sell unless they had the mark."

(Revelation 13:16-17)

This mark is not just about chips or currency—it is about ideology. The caste structure defines who is worthy and who is disposable. It is the economic engine of white supremacy and spiritual rebellion.

Mysterious Babylon, the eighth beast, will face judgment like Egypt, Rome, and colonial empires. Scripture says:

"We would have healed Babylon, but she is not healed. Forsake her... for her judgment reaches to the heavens."

(Jeremiah 51:9)

John saw Babylon fall in a single hour. The woman clothed in purple and scarlet, dripping with gold and blood, was drunk with the suffering of the oppressed:

"Babylon the Great... the mother of harlots and the abominations of the earth."

(Revelation 17:5)

This is the fall of every system built on bloodshed, lies, and greed—every structure that made skin color a curse and privilege a god.

Whether it is the Aryan caste system of the Vedas, the racism of the Roman church, or the economic brutality of colonialism, every beast will be judged. Every caste system will collapse. The time will come when the world can no longer hide behind patriotism, religious nationalism, or historical myths.

"Come out of her, My people, so you do not share in her sins or receive her plagues."

(Revelation 18:4)

In the end, justice is not optional—it is divine.

At the time of John's vision, five great empires had already fallen—Assyria, Babylon, Media, Persia, and Greece. Rome, the sixth beast, ruled the world. The seventh, Great Britain, inherited Rome's legacy, dominating Africa through colonization. From Britain came the United States, the eighth beast, carrying that same imperial spirit.

Revelation 19–20 foresees the fall of the beast and false prophet, the binding of Satan for a thousand years, and the resurrection of those martyred for Christ's truth. But after the millennium, Satan is released, and the final battle begins— Gog and Magog rise, sweeping nations, including Ethiopia and Libya, into a northern-led war.

Ezekiel and Daniel both foresaw this. Ethiopia, once a fierce defender against ancient colonial empires, would one day yield to northern powers. Once uncolonized, it is now weakened by war and famine. Daniel 11 warns of the North overpowering the South, seizing wealth and resources—reminding us that every empire's rise hides a deeper spiritual war.

"He will gain control of the treasures of gold and silver and all the riches of Egypt, with the Libyans and Nubians in submission."

(Daniel 11:43)

In Daniel 12, the prophet was told to seal the vision until the end. Ezekiel and John would later receive nearly identical revelations. Both describe rivers of healing water flowing from God's throne, trees bearing fruit, and leaves for the healing of nations. John writes:

"And there shall be no more curse, but the throne of God and the Lamb shall be in it... And His servants shall serve Him. They shall see His face, and His name shall be on their foreheads."

(Revelation 22:3 4)

Ezekiel and John saw not only judgment but restoration—the promise of healing after centuries of exploitation, conquest, and spiritual betrayal. This vision holds hope for all oppressed people, especially the descendants of Africa and the Afro-Semitic covenant people. Babylon may rise in power, but its fall is certain.

Mysterious Babylon, the final empire, is tied to a global caste system that thrives on racial inequality and white supremacy. The Bible warns of this final beast—a resurrected form of ancient empires—driven by military force, economic control, and spiritual deception.

"He causes all, both small and great, rich and poor, free and slave, to receive a mark... that no one may buy or sell except one who has the mark."

(Revelation 13:16-17)

This mark may symbolize casteism itself—the system that divides, labels, and oppresses people based on race, color, and origin. It is the legacy of empires, from Babylon to Rome to colonial Europe, and now to the modern powers of our time.

But the end of the story is not despair—it is justice. The beast, the false prophet, and Satan will be cast into the fire. The earth will be renewed, and the kingdom of God will restore what was broken. The river of life will flow again, and the oppressed will be healed. Those who resisted the mark, who stayed true despite persecution, will reign in righteousness.

The prophet Zechariah called the people to repentance, urging them to return to the Creator and finish rebuilding the Temple—a symbol of hope, healing, and covenant restoration. His message was not just about a physical structure, but about restoring the people's connection to divine purpose.

In a series of night visions, Zechariah saw that a new age was coming—one in which the Lord Himself would rise to fight for His scattered people and bring them home to Zion.

Zechariah pointed to a righteous leader, a messianic figure called the BRANCH, who would lead the rebuilding, not just of a temple made with hands, but of a covenant people broken by exile, oppression, and spiritual betrayal:

"Behold, the Man whose name is the BRANCH! From His place He shall branch out, and He shall build the temple of the Lord; yes, He shall build the temple of the Lord. He shall bear the glory and sit and rule on His throne; so, He shall be a priest on His throne, and the counsel of peace shall be between them both."

(Zechariah 6:12-13)

This promise is more than ancient prophecy—it is a declaration of resistance and a vision of Afro-Semitic liberation. The coming King would reject the trappings of empire—no military pride, no corrupt politics. He would enter lowly, riding on a donkey—a direct challenge to the Roman war horses and the oppressive systems of domination, caste, and white supremacy:

"Shout, O daughter of Jerusalem! Behold, your King is coming to you; He is just and having salvation, lowly and riding on a donkey, a colt, the foal of a donkey."

(Zechariah 9:9)

This prophecy foreshadows the arrival of Yeshua Ha'Mashiach—an Afro-Semitic liberator who would confront injustice not with violence, but with truth, humility, and a call to repentance. He was a revolutionary figure who overturned caste systems and stood with the oppressed, fulfilling Zechariah's vision in both word and deed.

Conclusion

What a journey it has been.

After more than 200 pages exploring the deep roots of racism, caste systems, colonial violence, and prophetic truth—from the ancient world to modern empires—we have reached the end of this book. But in reality, the work is far from over. This is not just a conclusion. It is a call to action.

The horrors we have examined—enslavement, apartheid, casteism, genocide, systemic racism, and the manipulation of religion to uphold white supremacy—did not begin in the 21st century. They are ancient sins with modern faces. From Babylon to the transatlantic and Indian Ocean slave trade, from Jim Crow to colorism in Bollywood and Africa, from

January 6th insurrections to no-knock warrants and racialized policing—the evil persists.

But so does resistance.

The scriptures repeatedly remind us that God hears the cries of the oppressed. The prophets warned us about nations that enrich themselves through bloodshed and deception. Revelation makes it clear that Mysterious Babylon, no matter how powerful, wealthy, or arrogant, will fall under the judgment of the Creator.

And yet, even in the midst of all this, the heart of the message is simple: justice, truth, and love.

It is not about skin color. It is about character. It is about dismantling a system that tells us one race, ethnicity, or culture is inherently better than another. It is about refusing to be complicit in white privilege or caste superiority, and choosing instead to walk in humility, equity, and truth.

Throughout this book, we have seen that not all white people choose evil. Some risked everything to challenge slavery, segregation, and systemic injustice. They were persecuted for it. That matters too, because it shows us that transformation is possible.

What the world needs now is not more religion without righteousness. It needs people of every color, class, and creed willing to stand up against corruption, call out the lies of supremacy, and walk in prophetic love.

I wrote this book not just to inform, but to awaken.

If you've read this far, I pray you leave with more than knowledge—I pray you leave with conviction, courage, and a renewed sense of purpose.

We are the generation tasked with tearing down the idols of caste and white supremacy. We are the ones called to prepare the way for justice and restoration.
Let the work begin.

Peace, love, and liberation—
Until Mysterious Babylon fall.

The End

Bibliography

Aboriginal Tasmanian. (2003, June 5). Wikipedia. http:// en.wikipedia. org/wiki/Tasmanian_Aborigines

Adkins, L. & Adkins, R.A. (1994). *Handbook to Life in Ancient Rome.* Oxford University

Press.

Africa Opposing Viewpoints. (2008). Greenhaven Press.*Alexander theGreat.*(n.d.).Carpenoctem. http://www.carpenoctem.tv/ military/ alex.html

AncientCivilization.(2000).Thinkquest.http://www.library. thinkquest.org/C004203/science/science02.htm

Ancient Mother of the Sudan and Ethiopia. (n.d.). Suite 101. http:// www. suite101.com/content/queen-candace-of-antiquity- al67567

Ancient Nubia: Map and History of Rulers. (n.d.). http://wysinger. homestead.com/mapofnubia.html

Anderson, S. (1995). *The Black Holocaust for Beginners.* Writer and
Readers Publishing, Inc.

Atlas of the Bible: An Illustrated Guide to the Holy Land. (1982).
Reader's Digest Association, Inc.

Babylon Empire. (n.d.). Livius. http://www.livius.org/ba-bd/
babylon/ babylonian_empire.html

Benson, C. (1970). *Supernatural Dreams and Visions.* Logos
International.

Bernstein, P. L. (2012). *The Power of Gold, The History of an
Obsession.* John Wiley & Sons, Inc.

Bishop, A. & Dunston, J. (1993). *The Black Man in the Old Testament
and Its World.*

Africa World Press, Inc.

Black War. (2004, February 27). Wikipedia. http://en.wikipedia.org/
wiki/BlackWar

Blight, D. *The Civil War and Reconstruction Era, 1845-1877: Lecture
10 Transcript.* Open Media. http://openmedia.yale.edu/projects/
iphone/ departments/hist/hist119/transcript10.html

Burton, K.A. (2007). *The Blessing of Africa.* InterVarsity Press.
Casson, L. (1981). *Treasures of the World, The Pharaohs.*
Stonehenge Press, Inc.

Ciment, J. (2001). *Atlas of African-American History.* Media Projects
Inc.

Civil Rights. (n.d.). Southern Connecticut State University. http://
www.southernct.edu/~ils69315/sixties/civilrights.htm

Clarke, J.H. (1998). *Christopher Columbus and the African Holocaust:
Slavery and the Rise of European Capitalism.* A&B Publisher
Group.

Costello, D. & Duvall, T. (2020, March 17). *How did Breonna Taylor
die? What to know about the Louisville woman shot by police.*

Courier Journal. https://www.courier-journal.com/story/news/
local/2020/05/12/breonna-taylor-case-what-know-louisville-
emt- killed-cops/3110066001/

Cummins, J. (2010). *The World's Bloodiest History: Massacre, Genocide, and Scars They Left on*
Civilization. Fair Winds Press.

Darwin, C. (1998). *The Descent of Man.* Prometheus Books.
Dawood, N.J. (1995). *The Koran.* The Penguin Group.

Debroy, B.D. (2011). *The Holy Vedas: Rig Veda Yajur Veda Sama Veda Atharva Veda.* B.R. Publishing Corporation.

Dionysus or Bacchus. (n.d.). In Depth Info. http://www.indepthinfo.com

Duncan, M.J. (2003). *The Complete Idiot's Guide to African American History.* Pearson
Education, Inc.

Dyer, C.H. (1995). *World News and Bible Prophecy.* Tyndale House Publishers.

Dyer, C.H. (2003). *The Rise of Babylon.* Moody Publishers.

Faal, C. *The Partition of Africa.* (2009, February 21). Black Past. http:// www.blackpast.org/?q=gah/partition-africa

Fagg, J.E. (1965). *Cuba, Haiti, and the Dominican Republic.* Prentice-Hall, Inc.

Feldman, G. (1999). *Politics, Society, And the Klan in Alabama.* The University of Alabama Press.

Finley, M.I. (1965). *Josephus: The Jewish War and other selections.* Twayne Publishers, Inc.

Fraley, B. (1984). *The Last Days in America.* Christian Life Publishers. Gaines, A. (1994). *Herodotus and the Explorers of the Classical Age.*
Chelsea House Publishers.

Gelb, N. (2010). *Kings of the Jews.* The Jewish Publication Society. Goddard, John. (2007, May 31). *Where Ancient Gods and Royalty Walked.*
The Toronto Star. https://www.thestar.com/news/2007/05/31/where_ancient_gods_and_royalty_walked.htm

Greenwood, S. (2006). *The Encyclopedia of Magic Witchcraft.*

Griffith, R.T.H. (2008). *The Rig Veda Complete.* Forgotten Books.
Hart, G. (2000). *Ancient Egypt.* Dorling Kindersley.

Hawass, Z. (2005). *Tutankhamun and the Golden Age of the Pharaohs.* Geographic Society.

Hill, J. (2010). *Herodotus on Cambyses.* Ancient Egypt Online. http://www.ancientegyptonline.co.uk/HerodCambyses.html

Hillel, D. (2006). *The Natural History of the Bible.* Columbia University Press.

Hirsch, J.S. (2002). *Riot And Remembrance: The Tulsa Race War and Its Legacy.* Houghton Mifflin Company.

Hislop, R.A. (1959). *The Two Babylons.* Loizeaux Brothers, Inc.
Hitchcock, M. (1999). *The Complete Book of Bible Prophecy.* Tyndale House Publishers.

Hitchcock, M. (2003). *The Second Coming of Babylon.* Multnomah Publishers, Inc.

Houston, D.D. (2007). *Wonderful Ethiopians of the Ancient Cushite Empire.* BiblioBazaar.

Jackson, J.G. (2001). *Introduction to African Civilizations.* Kensington Publishing Corp.

Jensen, I.L. (1981). *Jensen's Survey of the New Testament.* The Moody Bible Institute.

Jeremiah, D.D. (2010). *The Coming Economic Armageddon.* NavPress Publishing Group.

Jugurtha. (2002, December 13). Wikipedia. http://en.wikipedia.org/wiki/Jugurtha

Hazleton, L. (2007). *Jezebel, The Untold Story of the Bible's Harlot Queen.* Doubleday Broadway Publishing Group.

Herodotus. (1982). The Persian War, Shepherd, W. (Trans.). Cambridge University Press.

Karimi, F. (2020, August 28). *Kenosha shooting suspect called a friend to say he 'killed somebody,' police say, and then shot two others.* CNN. https://www.cnn.com/2020/08/28/us/kyle-rittenhouse-kenosha- shooting/index.html

Khan, S.M. (2007). *The Shallow Graves Of Rwanda*. I.B. Tauris Publishers.

Kosof, A. (1989). *The Civil Rights Movement and Its Legacy*. Franklin Watts.

Loewen, J.W. (2007). *Lies My Teacher Told Me: Everything Your American History* Textbook Got Wrong—The New Press.

Mark P.L. & Silberman, N.A. (1995). *Invisible America: Unearthing Our Hidden History*. Henry Holt and Company, Inc.

McKissack, P.A. (1987). *The Civil Rights Movement in America: From 1865 to the Present*. Regensteiner Publishing Enterprises, Inc.

Millmore, M. (2007). *Imagining Egypt*. Black Dog and Leventhal Publishers, Inc.

Napata. (2005, June 6). Wikipedia. http://en.wikipedia.org/wiki/Napata

Newton, John. (2010). *Thoughts Upon the African Slave Trade*. https://cowperandnewtonmuseum.org.uk/wp-content/uploads/2020/07/thoughts-upon-african-slave-trade-john-newton.pdf

Noss, D.S. (1999). *A History of the World's Religions, 10th Edition*. Prentice-Hall, Inc.

One of Africa's best-kept secrets. (n.d). BBC. https://www.bbc.com/news/ world-africa

Packard, J.M. *American Nightmare: The History of Jim Crow*. New York: St. Martin's Press, 2002.

Packer, J.I. (1995). *Nelson's Illustrated Encyclopedia of Bible Facts*. Thomas Nelson, Inc.

Pike, A. (2010). *The Aryan Race: Country, Character, and Manners of The Indo-Aryans*. Kessinger Publishing.

Psamtik I. (2004, January 27). Wikipedia. http://en.wikipedia.org/wiki/ Psamtik I

Punic Wars. (2001, October 17). Wikipedia. en.wikepedia.org/wiki/Punic wars

Rediker, M. (2007). *The Slave Ship, A Human History*. Penguin Group, Inc.

Remembering Martin Luther King, Jr. (n.d.). Black Americans. http://www.blackamericans.com/black-history/black-history

Rodgers, N. (2006). *Ancient Rome.* Hermes House.

RomanSpain.(n.d.).CitytoursBarcelonia.http://www.citytoursbarcelona.com/roman_spain.html

SennacheribPrism.(n.d.).BibleDudes. http://bibledudes.com/bilical-studies/finds/prismtranslation.php

Sennacherib: the Year–701.(2012). Varchive. http://www.varchive.org/ tac/701.htm

Slavery In Ancient Rome. (n.d.). Rich East. http://www.richeast.org/htwn/Greeks/Romans/slavery/slavery2.html/

Smith, R. & Jones, S.L. (2000). *The Prentice Hall Anthology of African American Literature.* Prentice Hall, Inc.

Spiegel, M. (1996). *The Dreaded Comparison: Human and Animal Slavery.* Mirror Books/I.D.E.A.

Spielvogel, J.J. (2005). *World History Modern Times.* National Geographic Society.

Splendors Of The Past: Lost Cities of the Ancient World. (1981). National Geographic Society.

Statue of Liberty. (2001, October 22). Wikipedia. http://en.wikipedia. org/wiki/Statue_of_Liberty

Tantamani. (2004, November 2). Wikipedia. http://en.wikipedia.org/ wiki/Tantamani

Temple of Artemis. (2010). Ephesus. http://www.ephesus.ws/temple-of- artemis.html

The Carnival Celebration that Became Christmas & New

New Year's Eve. (n.d.). Saturnalia. http://www. carnaval.com/saturnalia

The Hanging Gardens of Babylon. (n.d.). Ocean Baby. http:// www.ocean-baby.com/

The History of Herodotus. (n.d.). Classic MIT. http://classic.mit.edu/Herotodus/history.html

The Holy Bible, New King James Version. (1992). Thomas Nelson, Inc.

The Kushite conquest of Palestine and the 'Assyro-Kushite Wars.' (n.d.) AncientSudan. http://www.ancientsudan.org/history_07_assyro. htm

The Urantia Book. (1995). Urantia Foundation.

The World Book Encyclopedia. (1991). World Book, Inc.

The World's Last Mysteries. (1981). Reader's Digest Association.

Third Punic War. (n.d.) UNRV Roman History. http://www.unrv. com/ empire/third-punic-war.php

Wagman, R.J. (1993). *The Supreme Court: A Citizen's Guide.* Pharos Books.

Walvoord, J.F & Zuck, R.B. (1983). *Bible Knowledge Commentary: New Testament.* David C. Cook.

Wilson, A. (1997). *Paul: The Mind of the Apostle.* W.W. Norton & Company.

Windsor, R.R. (2003). *From Babylon to Timbuktu.* Windsor Golden Series.

Wintz, C.D. (2007). *Harlem Speaks: A Living History of the Harlem Renaissance.* Sourcebooks.

Youngblood, R.F., Bruce, F.F., Nelson, T. & Harrison, R.K. (1995). Nelson's New Illustrated Bible Dictionary. Thomas Nelson, Inc.

About the Author

Michael Ray Lemons is an insightful and uncompromising author whose works challenge readers to confront the forces that shape human history, society, and the spirit. With a sharp focus on power, race, and faith, Lemons weaves together historical research, cultural analysis, and prophetic insight to expose the systems—both ancient and modern—that sustain oppression and resist liberation.

His body of work spans genres but remains unified by a single purpose: to reveal truth and inspire change.

Trapped Between Two Worlds: The Angel Without Wings – A compelling spiritual narrative exploring faith, inner conflict, and the struggle between light and darkness, following an angel's journey through a world both beautiful and unforgiving.

The Esau Effect: Reshaping the World in the Act of War – A critical examination of how war and the pursuit of dominance have historically reshaped global power structures, economies, and ideologies.

Cush to Mysterious Babylon: Africa and the Covenant People – An exploration of Africa's historical and spiritual significance, connecting the legacy of ancient civilizations to the biblical "Covenant People," and reframing Africa's role in global history.

Kush to Mysterious Babylon: The History of the Hindu Caste & White Privilege (2nd Edition) – An expanded and deeply researched work drawing parallels between the Hindu caste system and white supremacy, linking both to a global history of systemic oppression. This edition broadens the scope to include colonization, resistance movements, and the prophetic call for justice.

Lemons' writing is unapologetically rooted in an Afrocentric perspective, combining scholarship and storytelling to challenge mainstream narratives. His work is as much a call to accountability as it is a celebration of resilience—urging readers to recognize the deep connections between past injustices and present struggles, and to take part in the ongoing fight for truth, equity, and liberation.

www.ingramcontent.com/pod-product-compliance
Lightning Source LLC
Chambersburg PA
CBHW050854150626
46549CB00013B/1673